Praise for *If the Buddha Got Stuck*

"Being stuck and feeling you have no way out is an inevitable part of life. Whether you are stuck in a bad relationship, a job going nowhere, a midlife funk or a self-defeating pattern, *If the Buddha Got Stuck* provides a roadmap to freedom and greater possibilities.... Encouraging, practical, beautifully written."

> —Laura Davis, author of *I Thought We'd Never Speak Again*
> and coauthor of *The Courage to Heal*

"As Gandhi so aptly put it: 'We must become the change we wish to see in the world.' Charlotte Kasl's new book overflows with insight, humor and eminently practical suggestions for how to do just that.... This book takes us to the true source of world peace—the individual human heart freed from fears and limiting beliefs."

> —Anita Doyle, former director of the Jeannette Rankin
> Peace Center, Missoula, Montana

"If you have suspected wisdom lurked in Eastern teachings, but found the language impenetrable ... if previous attempts to work with your life from a Western philosophical or psychological perspective encountered gaps that did not let you leap to your personal solutions ... then *If the Buddha Got Stuck* (which he was before he gained the insights we find so useful and inspiring) just might be your bridge to some life-changing insights."

> —Rowan Conrad, Ph.D., director, Open Way Mindfulness
> Center

"Kasl provides inspiration to go deeper, reach higher, let go of internal critics, and feel the aliveness of who we truly are. Whether recovering from an addiction, feeling depressed, or wanting more joy, *If the Buddha Got Stuck* brings perspective, inspiring stories, and useful exercises to feel less overwhelmed by life's difficulties."

> —Lisa M. Najavits, Ph.D., associate professor of psychiatry,
> Harvard Medical School and author of *Seeking Safety:
> A Treatment Manual for PTSD and Substance Abuse*

IF THE BUDDHA GOT STUCK

Charlotte Sophia Kasl, Ph.D., a practicing psychotherapist, workshop leader for twenty-eight years, and bestselling author, has had longtime connections to feminism, Buddhism, Quaker practice, and Reiki healing. She has written extensively on relationships, joy, sexuality, healing, and addiction, weaving together many aspects of spirituality and psychology to bring a holistic, empowering approach to all her work. Her books include *If the Buddha Dated; If the Buddha Married; Finding Joy; Many Roads, One Journey; Women, Sex, and Addiction; A Home for the Heart;* and *Yes, You Can! A Guide to Empowerment Groups.* Formerly of Minneapolis, Minnesota, Kasl now lives in an octagonal house near Missoula, Montana, where she writes and has a psychotherapy practice.

ALSO BY CHARLOTTE KASL

If the Buddha Dated: A Handbook for Finding Love on a Spiritual Path
If the Buddha Married: Creating Enduring Relationships on a Spiritual Path
Finding Joy: 101 Ways to Free Your Spirit and Dance with Life
Many Roads, One Journey: Moving Beyond the Twelve Steps
Women, Sex, and Addiction: A Search for Love and Power
A Home for the Heart: Creating Intimacy with Loved Ones, Neighbors, and Friends
Yes, You Can! A Guide to Empowerment Groups

IF THE BUDDHA GOT STUCK

A Handbook for Change on a Spiritual Path

CHARLOTTE SOPHIA KASL, PH.D.

PENGUIN COMPASS

PENGUIN BOOKS
Published by the Penguin Group
Penguin Group (USA) Inc., 375 Hudson Street, New York, New York 10014, U.S.A.
Penguin Group (Canada), 90 Eglinton Avenue East, Suite 700, Toronto, Ontario,
    Canada M4P 2Y3 (a division of Pearson Penguin Canada Inc.)
Penguin Books Ltd, 80 Strand, London WC2R 0RL, England
Penguin Ireland, 25 St Stephen's Green, Dublin 2, Ireland
    (a division of Penguin Books Ltd)
Penguin Group (Australia), 250 Camberwell Road, Camberwell, Victoria 3124,
    Australia (a division of Pearson Australia Group Pty Ltd)
Penguin Books India Pvt Ltd, 11 Community Centre, Panchsheel Park,
    New Delhi – 110 017, India
Penguin Group (NZ), 67 Apollo Drive, Rosedale, North Shore 0632, New Zealand
    (a division of Pearson New Zealand Ltd)
Penguin Books (South Africa) (Pty) Ltd, 24 Sturdee Avenue,
    Rosebank, Johannesburg 2196, South Africa

Penguin Books Ltd, Registered Offices: 80 Strand, London WC2R 0RL, England

First published in Penguin Books 2005

Page 241 constitutes an extension of this copyright page.

LIBRARY OF CONGRESS CATALOGING-IN-PUBLICATION DATA
Kasl, Charlotte Davis.
    If the Buddha got stuck : a handbook for change on a spiritual path / by Charlotte
    Sophia Kasl.
        p. cm.
    ISBN 978-0-14-219628-1
    1. Religious life—Buddhism. I. Title.
    BQ4302.K37 2005
    294.3'444—dc22   2004053396

Set in Albertina MT with Village Titling • Designed by Sabrina Bowers

Dedicated to

The Jeanette Rankin Peace Center of Missoula, Montana

and Peace Makers everywhere . . .
Who seek to bring together
all that is fragmented
and separated and hurting
in the world
between us and within us.

To those who seek to understand,
create connections,
reconnect,
reach out in kindness,
share resources,
create equality and justice
and see in the eyes of people everywhere
that we are all brothers and sisters made of one creator.

Namaste

A Note on the Title

What do you mean, "If the Buddha got stuck"?

Of course the Buddha didn't get stuck. What a ridiculous idea. Buddha literally means being awake or conscious, and you can't be awake and asleep at the same time.

The Buddha wasn't a Buddhist either. He was a man, formerly known as Siddhartha Gautama, who, after many years of seeking the cause of suffering, became enlightened. That is, he broke through his identity as a separate self to live at one with the energy of All That Is. People started referring to him as The Buddha when he became a teacher who was clearly awake and at peace with himself.

The title really asks, what if you got stuck, and looked to Buddhist teachings, to help you get unstuck and feel more at ease in the world? What if you really believed that there are specific ways to ease your stress, calm your fears, gather courage to take action, and bring greater peace and happiness to your life? It is possible. The Buddha found the way, and his teachings can help you regardless of your background, religion, or belief system.

Welcome to the Journey.

Heartfelt Thanks and Bright Blessings . . .

To my longtime agent Edite Kroll, for humor, availability, encouragement, faith, good conversations, and help with the manuscript. It's amazing to me that seventeen years have gone by since you took my first book proposal.

To Janet Goldstein, for encouragement, suggestions, excellent editing, and staying steady with this project, even though it took much longer than expected.

To Billie Fitzpatrick, my "book doctor," for stellar help at every level—organization, focusing ideas, making better transitions, and encouragement when it seemed like a daunting task.

Special thanks to teacher and friend Stephen Wolinsky, for books, workshops, and conversations on quantum consciousness, advaita vendata, and Buddhism. You "get it" and "are it" more than anyone else I know. I appreciate my endless experiences of dropping into the void as a result of the processes I did in forty-six days of your life-changing workshops. I greatly appreciate your clear and focused feedback on this book, arising from your deep comprehension of Buddhism, along with your unmitigated honesty, availability, friendliness, and great sense of humor.

Thanks in memoriam to Ken Keyes and the Cornucopia community I attended in 1980. This was my introduction to Buddhism with the concept that our suffering is a result of our attachments and, what seemed like a vague concept at the time, that everything is one energy. You set me on a new path.

Heartfelt thanks to the following people who have given interviews, input, guidance, support, friendship, inspiration, and suggestions . . . in no particular order: Laura Davis, Marilyn Beech, Sheila

Jaya Lindquist, Helen and Jack Watkins, Shabda Kahn, Sigurd Hoppe, Jackie Kurtz, Zamilla ra, Carol Narrance, Kristie Hager, Pat Bik, Suzie Risho, Lindsey Bailey, Audrey Campbell, Kristina Smucker, Pamela Stoneham, Kate Wenninger, Ed Shope, Jerry Moss, Bruce Barret, Adair Canter, Steven Hesla, Margaret Baldrige, Karen Tacke, Starshine, David James Duncan, and all the people in the writing class, especially Stephanie Walkinshaw and Azita Osanlou, all the friendly people at Weight Watchers, and all the other people who provided inspiration for this book. Thanks also to the brave and courageous clients who have taught me so much and daily affirm the incredible capacity we have for healing.

Contents

STEP THREE:
PAY ATTENTION

STEP FOUR:
LIVE IN REALITY, LISTEN TO YOUR TRUTHS

STEP FIVE:
CONNECT WITH OTHERS, CONNECT WITH LIFE

STEP SIX:
MOVE FROM THOUGHT TO ACTION

STEP SEVEN:
LET GO

Introduction:
A Personal Story of Getting Stuck and Unstuck

Over a decade ago I broke free from a settled, secure life in Minneapolis for a financially uncertain existence amid the staggering beauty of the mountains, rivers, and hiking trails of Montana. Feeling agitated by the city with its constant speed and noise, cramped on my forty-foot lot, I hungered for space, starry nights, watching the sun rise, and the cool mountain mornings of summer. I wanted to sit down at night and play the piano at my ease without the creepy feeling of unseen ears lurking around me.

My sister's sudden death a few years earlier had acutely reminded me of our precious, finite lives. Five years before she died, we had had one of our last special visits after she had driven with me from Minnesota to take possession of my magical octagonal house, perched on ten acres above the Missoula valley in Montana.

I felt at home amid huge old ponderosa pines with a panoramic view of the mountains. I relished watching the sun and the moon rise as the streams of light and shadows in the house traveled north and south through the seasons. At first I was able to balance my time between morning walks, writing, presenting workshops, my psychotherapy practice, playing the piano, and exploring the vast terrain with friends.

But several years later, I increasingly felt squeezed by publication deadlines. Writing, once my creative pleasurable union with the muses, became adulterated by pressure, especially on those beautiful, clear, blue-sky Montana summer days when I longed to be in the mountains rather than staring at them over my computer screen. Three years earlier, I had promised myself I wouldn't write in July and August, but there I was, doing exactly what I promised myself I wouldn't do. The familiar symptoms of being stuck emerged.

I started eating too much chocolate and gaining weight as I watched the occasional bird come to the feeder on the deck off my writing room. I started skipping physical therapy following knee surgery, not spending time with friends, taking walks, or playing the piano. How could I do this to myself? My health, my weight, my happiness were all sliding away.

The discord between my life and my dream crashed together on a Monday in August. I awoke, sunlight streaming on the bed, a chirping squirrel near my window promising a beautiful day. Euphoria gave way to despair when I remembered the looming deadline. A voice inside was shouting, "I hate myself, I hate my life, I'm doing what I said I would never do again. I'm writing in August. I'm always showing up late to gatherings and leaving early, driven by a deadline." I sat bolt upright, invigorated by this clear, truthful alarm. But a dreary thought argued back: "If I'm going to meet the deadline, I have to write all day . . . and all this week, and all next week. What is life for?" I thought of August slipping away.

A knot tightened in my stomach as I remembered that this was the first day of the International Choral Festival, a glorious once-in-three-years event, at which over thirty choirs from all over the world bring an array of culture, tradition, and music to our little town. After having missed most of the performances three years before while I was writing, I had vowed that this time I'd clear my calendar and make the rounds of the parks, churches, and shopping malls to hear the various choirs throughout the week. Instead, here I was again—torn and guilty.

I called my agent.

"There's too much pressure. I want to change the publication date," I said. She kindly pointed out that I should try to get the book out for Valentine's Day and gently urged me to believe I could.

Like a reverberating chant, I heard myself saying, "I don't care. I don't care about the number of books we sell. I don't care about the money. I don't care if we get better publicity if it comes out in February. I don't care! I care about my knee, my health, my life, and the pleasure I once felt from writing."

As my voice got more desperate, a charge of energy welled up inside me like a volcano about to erupt. For a moment I hovered between pushing it down or letting it rise. It broke through and tears exploded: "I can't do it all. I hate myself. I promised I would never do this to myself again," I said, sobbing. "We have to change the publication date."

It was as if a strong wind had blown away the dissonance inside. I was aware of breathing again. I realized that ultimately I could make a choice even if it meant a lot of people would be disappointed or even angry at me. It's my life, I kept thinking to myself.

After a long pause my agent said softly, "Of course."

Later that afternoon, my editor called back, a friendly smile in her voice. "I heard the news," she said. "I'm calling with encouragement and support. We can change the publication date. It will be a wonderful book."

In the late afternoon, feeling the elation of someone who had just graduated or gotten out of prison, I arrived at Bonner Park with a large green folding chair, a roasted chicken from Safeway, romaine lettuce, and a *New Yorker* magazine. I planted myself front row center of the band shell and relished the sight of people gathering at the park with their chairs, blankets, and picnic paraphernalia, ready to enjoy the music. I read, well, mostly looked at *New Yorker* cartoons, ambled around, chatted with friends, and finally settled in to hear the singing—most notably the Cuban Exude chorus, with their colorful, tightly woven harmonies and rhythms. Later, at home, I sat on my deck drinking tea, watching the first stars appear.

Several days later, having enjoyed concerts, walks, and spending time with friends, the writing muses invited me back with clarity and pleasure. With the pressure gone, I relaxed at the computer, feeling back in my own life.

I would keep the promise to myself. The book would get written and I would have a life.

Welcome to the Journey

The purpose of life is to be alive. Not to gather objects, achieve, accumulate successes, or forge your body to fit a mold. It's simply to be alive. To touch, feel, sense, hear, see, and live in a dynamic flow of whatever arises in the moment; to accept the wild and crazy thoughts that go through your mind, your animal nature, your wisdom, the fears that arise and grip your chest, the laughter that brings tears, and the joy that takes you beyond yourself. To be alive is to meet and accept every part of yourself—the scuzzy, sweet, passionate, talented, or slow. From this place of self-acceptance you can be a good friend to yourself and others.

This does not preclude achieving, learning, or taking good care of yourself, but you do so because your body, mind, and energy converge to do whatever feels in harmony with the aliveness that you are.

From this point of self-acceptance our consciousness spills over into the vast expanse of human experience and we start to see the connections between all sentient life, between our brothers and sisters everywhere. Said another way, we start to experience love.

This book is about the journey from being stuck to unstuck, from feeling trapped to being free; from compromising our values to living at one with our integrity; from being immersed in thoughts from the past to living in the present. It's a process and a journey that sometimes starts with a dull ache and other times with acute pain. It's sometimes motivated by survival needs and other times by the thought, "There's got to be more than this." Some people are visited by grace with a mind-opening experience that leads them to realize there is a whole different way to live, and becoming more open and at ease becomes a touchstone for life.

Getting unstuck is not a one-time endeavor because, as the moon waxes and wanes, life's natural experiences of loss and change repeatedly challenge us to let go, shift our perceptions, and bring new ideas and plans into our lives. A pulsing, flowing life is about letting go in hundreds of ways to allow for something new. Sometimes getting unstuck feels like pushing through fear. Other times it's more like leaping off a cliff. And still other times you just sit with whatever is going on inside, neither expressing nor repressing it.

Becoming unstuck is about becoming free. My hope in writing this book is to encourage you to explore wherever you feel stuck—bored, scared, protective, petty, exhausted, afraid, or unfulfilled—and to believe you can have a much more satisfying life. You can make both the small, daily changes that will bring more spark and flow into your life and the bigger changes, both internally and externally, that can shift the whole landscape of your existence.

It's incredibly easy to get stuck in life. Whether we're just starting out, building a career, nurturing a family, in the throes of falling in or out of love, the increasing pace and pressures of life, economic uncertainty, and the constant seduction to believe that more stuff or more activity equals more happiness can trap us emotionally and financially. And many of us feel trapped not only by the demands of the present but also by the pull of the past. We've developed physical patterns of becoming rigid, tense, afraid. We have all kinds of critics and nay-sayers intruding in our minds, fighting against our best intentions and making us feel guilty or inadequate. It's no wonder that getting unstuck and breaking free can feel like swimming against the current.

People often talk about how hard it is to change. It is and it isn't. Change requires deep questioning, internal shifts, giving up the known, and often the images of who we think we are. But many acts of change—the small shifts and first steps that can add up to something much bigger—can be surprisingly easy. And *not* changing is even harder. Think about it. What does it cost you to constantly censor the parts of you that want to stretch, adventure, and express themselves? How does staying in a rut affect your body, heart, and mind? What regrets would you have if today were your last?

So go ahead—let yourself dream. Allow yourself to imagine what life might be like if it had more personal meaning for you. If you switched careers, took up something you've fantasized about, or went more deeply into your relationships. When you let yourself say, "Enough, I'm willing to take a step," you have begun the journey.

> *You must be the change you wish to see in the world.*
> —MAHATMA GANDHI

The changes we make for ourselves are outwardly reflected in our world. Becoming unstuck in life and being a force for good in the world are inseparable. Our friendliness, concern for others, welcoming smiles, and ability to listen and embrace others without judgment contribute to a peaceful world. As we become more at ease with ourselves and more passionately involved with whatever fulfills us, our focus naturally expands to our families, friends, communities, and our world. Becoming unstuck becomes both an individual and community effort with each affecting the other. In Buddhist terms, as we recognize our own suffering, we recognize the suffering of the world we live in. We come to see our lives as part of the larger whole.

Siddhartha Gautama, who later became known as the Buddha, embarked on a quest to understand the cause of suffering. Was Siddhartha ever stuck? To the extent that he kept focused on his overriding desire to find the cause of suffering, he was not stuck. He did, however, take some dead-end turns and was temporarily stuck many times. But in every situation he acknowledged something wasn't working and tried another path. The steps to change found in this book echo his journey.

Siddhartha was born around 563 B.C. in Nepal, of wealthy parents who ruled a small kingdom. He married at the age of sixteen to a neighboring princess, Yasodhara, and they had one son, Rahula. Houston Smith, in *World Religions*, describes the legend of The Four Passing Sights that stirred Siddhartha to renounce his luxurious life in search of a spiritual path:

"When Siddhartha was born his father summoned fortune tellers to discern his future. All agreed this was no usual child, but his career was crossed with an ambiguity. If he succeeded his father, he would unify India and become a world conqueror, but if he forsook the world he would become a world redeemer. His father wanted the former destiny, so he spared no effort to keep his son on course. Palaces and dancing girls were placed at his disposal, and orders were given that no unpleasantness be allowed into his courtly life. When he left the palace, runners were stationed to clear the roads of the old, the diseased, and the dead."

One day, however, curious and intrigued by the outside world, Siddhartha slipped past his father's control, left the palace, and roamed the nearby streets. On successive occasions he saw an old man, gaunt and trembling as he leaned on his staff, a man riddled with disease, a dead man lying by the road, and then a monk with a shaven head, orange robe and begging bowl who told Siddhartha of a path of renouncing the world.

Siddhartha, stirred by these images of illness, poverty, and abstinence from earthly gains, was increasingly drawn to understand the causes of suffering. As Houston Smith writes, "The abundance of his palace life ceased to satisfy, and he decided to leave to become a truth-seeker. He left his sleeping wife and child during the night, rode away, left his horse, shaved his head and put on the ochre robe."

In the following six years he studied with Hindu masters, then joined a group of ascetics who sought enlightenment through self-deprecation and renunciation. After nearly dying of starvation from these extreme practices, Siddhartha became aware that they were not taking him closer to the truth he sought. He realized that one could become as attached to austerity as to material wealth or the pleasures of the senses. From that point on he espoused the middle way—living simply, without leaning toward material, emotional, or mental extremes.

In the last phase of his search, Siddhartha Gautama concentrated on forms of meditation and yogic practices, but he still had not found the complete answer to his question. Then instead of looking further or hoping to find answers outside himself, he sat down under the Bodhi tree with the feeling that the wisdom he was seeking was near.

Houston Smith continues, "Days later, in the early morning, as the stars glittered in the eastern sky, his mind pierced the world's bubble, his identity as Siddhartha collapsed into and was restored with the effulgence of true being. The Great Awakening had Arrived. Over time he became known as The Buddha, which means the one who is awake."

The Buddha resisted all attempts by others to make him into a god or deity; rather, he encouraged all people to awaken to their Buddha nature. Buddhism became a path of learning through experience—if you don't truly know something in your heart and reflect it in the way you live, you don't yet know it fully. The Buddha was active as a teacher, and his life became a model of balance between teaching and retreating into solitude, which he did periodically throughout his days and for three months out of every year.

The steps in this book parallel the Buddha's journey.

The first step is to be aware of your unrest, unhappiness, and longing for something richer, more balanced and meaningful. The second is to Show Up for life in a myriad of ways. With curiosity and fascination, go beyond your prescribed life and explore the world beyond your usual rituals, beliefs, and habits—bringing electricity and spark to your life, challenging yourself, having fun, meeting new situations. You might sign up for a class, travel to a place you've never been, go to a lecture on an unfamiliar topic, seek counseling, or take a day off for pure pleasure.

You may not know why you are pulled in a certain direction, but you let yourself follow it, having new adventures, doing things in different ways. Siddhartha never would have become intrigued about suffering if he hadn't slipped out of the palace and seen the poverty-stricken people on the road. He didn't have a particular agenda; he was simply curious. By showing up and exploring new avenues, you open yourself to new possibilities.

In the third step, Pay Attention, you go deeper into the experience of inner self-awareness on a moment to moment, daily basis. Your senses and body are attuned more deeply, you listen more carefully, and your hearing becomes more nuanced.

You pay attention at many levels. You notice when you are tense, afraid, hungry, tired, or in need of comfort. You attune to what energizes and delights you, as opposed to what drains or feels lifeless to you. You notice when you want to be with others and when you seek solitude. Paying attention is grounded in the body and expressed through these questions: "Does this feel right for me?" "What do I really want to do?" "What is my body telling me?"

You also start to notice your mind—how opposing voices argue, censor, judge, and reel off the same stories day after day. You become aware of the allegiance you pay to rules and beliefs—being nice is good, angry is bad, you should never talk back, you can't do that—and start to notice the limitations these thoughts create.

Step four, Live in Reality, is about sorting out the past from the present. Is this flare of anger connected to my childhood or is it appropriate to this current situation? Am I feeling relaxed and clear—like a grownup—or am I uneasy and afraid like a child? Am I seeing that person for who he is, or as a stand-in for someone else? We ask ourselves, What is really true? Truth and integrity shine together in this stage, opening the door to deeper and more spontaneous, enjoyable relationships.

Step five, Connect with Others, lies at the heart of our journey. Genuine connections ease anxiety and help assuage our essential aloneness. They provide the secure base from which we can venture into scary places, celebrate our joys, and take risks, knowing someone is there to either cheer for us or catch us if we fall.

In step six, Take Action, we move from thinking to doing. Taking action becomes the process of how you live on a daily basis—from taking care of your body to signing up for a class, completing tasks, speaking up when someone is hurting you, getting out of bed early to take a walk, watering the plants before they wilt, throwing away the excess stuff that clutters your life. It's about movement, flow, energy, shifting, and shaking up the status quo. It's about becoming more of who you truly are.

The final step, Let Go, means that we stop grasping at all that is temporal—mind, thoughts, body, life situation—and experience being one with aliveness that penetrates all things. Instead of being the "doer" we become an expression of life that flows through us. From this relaxed place creative ideas and clear answers will often arise and help you come out of confusion and longing and make the desired changes in your life.

This journey requires a readiness to be altered, surprised, and sometimes astonished. If you bring this willingness to these steps you will open the way to breaking free and getting unstuck. Everyone can do it—it's a matter of following a well-tested path and persevering.

Buddhism and Self Help!

It may seem like a paradox to write a self help book from a Buddhist perspective. After all, Buddhism centers on transcending the self or the ego, not puffing it up or making it more concrete. Yet, as is often taught, you study the self in order to let go of the self. This book will help you realize the difference between self-absorption—the inflated ego—and self-awareness, which helps you to become conscious of the rise and fall of your thoughts, feelings, sensations, and desires. It will help you make connections about what creates tension and what allows ease, what brings happiness and what keeps you restless or detached.

Self-awareness has an expansive quality. It's about observing and being highly attuned to the interrelationship of your thoughts, body sensations, and external events—like watching a passing show with a sense of amusement. Self-absorption, on the other hand, is serious, contracts our energy, has a false sense of importance, and keeps us walled off in our separate identity.

Some books teach that you can get anything you want, if you "believe in yourself" and make great effort. The Buddhist path is about getting past the turmoil and stress created by your demands and expectations so you can experience the natural essence of who you are. It's not about making yourself feel bigger or gaining status or possessions; it's about freeing yourself to be happy, receptive, and open. From this place, answers to life's questions often arise spontaneously.

Many Eastern spiritual traditions include steps to follow on the path. The Buddha outlined eight steps for mindful, conscious living, which departed from those that came from his Hindu roots. The steps in this book build on each other and prepare you for the final chapter on letting go. So remember, while I include things the "self" can do, it's always with the understanding that it's a choice, and not a crucial one. It's there for the taking in the interest of clearing out whatever blocks the way to becoming happier, more at ease, and more fully who you are. These steps are not intended to become another list of rules to trigger guilt, shoulds, rigidity, or an inner competition, but as a path to freedom. Whether you follow them or not, you are and always have been one with the essence of all life.

Feel Your Longing, Notice Where You're Stuck

1. Notice the Roots of Uneasiness or Being Stuck

Lose yourself
Escape from the black cloud that surrounds you
Then you will see your own light,
as radiant as the full moon.

—RUMI, "IN THE ARMS OF THE BELOVED"

I'm going crazy in this relationship," Angie said to me, her lanky body stretched out on the chair in my office. "I'm obsessed over Jack. I think our relationship is pretty good one minute, and the next minute I think it's hopeless. My emotions come up and overwhelm me—I just dissolve and start crying. I keep questioning myself: am I being unreasonable? Expecting too much? Too judgmental? Or is he not for me? I get so confused trying to figure it out." She took a deep breath and smiled. "I drive myself nuts."

Experiencing endless turmoil in relationships is perhaps one of the deepest and most disturbing forms of being stuck. It stresses the mind, spirit, and body. Easing your relationship turmoil so you can have companionship, intimacy, and joy is for many a major part of getting unstuck.

For Matt, a malaise about work and recent relationships was what stood out. "I can't figure out what I want to do for a living, or a career," Matt said in a flat voice. "Everything I like doing doesn't pay, like taking troubled kids for summer camp trips and hikes, or working in a book store. Nothing seems to excite me." He went on to tell about two relationships that had fallen apart, well, mostly just faded away into boredom. Without access to his emotions, Matt had no internal thermostat to signal what brought joy, excitement, or stimulation. Getting his life unstuck required a tenacious willingness to stay with his feelings and learn to recognize the fear that lay under his habit of disconnecting.

For Margie and Bob, the stuck place came from the overwhelming stress they experienced as two professional working parents with two young rambunctious boys. Married for eight years, life had turned into "stress city," as Margie put it. "We weren't spending enough time with the children. We were always rushing around to get things done, and our nerves were often frayed—we'd start snapping at each other or feel depressed." "It wasn't how I wanted to live, either," Bob commented in his easy drawl. "We could do it, but life wasn't fun, and it sure wasn't good for the kids."

Long ago Margie and Bob had promised each other that life never was to be put on the shelf, so they decided to simplify life, live frugally, and have one parent stay at home until the children were in school.

Their move to action was a team effort that involved cutting expenses and taking on do-it-yourself projects—growing a vegetable garden and re-roofing their house themselves so they could afford a vacation, and taking bike trips and going camping as affordable vacations, which they did willingly to have the lifestyle they wanted. They learned how to have a lot of fun without spending much money. "And besides, I like yard sales, and don't want to be attached to stuff," Margie added. "If it's cheap we don't worry about it breaking or getting lost."

Their story sounds easy, but it required planning, budgeting, reigning in their impulses, and, most of all, working together. Margie and Bob did not feel deprived; they spoke of the wonderful freedom they experienced in terms of time, relaxation, and family closeness.

These stories illustrate three central arenas in which people get stuck—relationships, jobs/careers, and high-stress living. If you take each of them apart you will see that they are different in nature but have some underlying commonalities. Your primary stuck places tend to take center stage in your life. Until they are addressed they make it difficult to feel at ease or immersed in life. For Angie and Matt the stuck places were deeply rooted and spilled over into all aspects of their lives. With Margie and Bob, it was more of a problem-solving endeavor because they had already become free of many of the attachments that keep people stuck.

If you think about what you are longing for, the dreams and hopes you've had for your life, you might immediately be aware of areas in which you are stuck. What's out of sync? What feels disappointing? What are the thoughts that constantly go through your head about what you "should" be doing for yourself? What action do you avoid taking? How much of your energy is drained away worrying about a relationship, a stressful job, or feeling unhappy? Really listen to yourself.

2. Let Your Body Be Your Guide

The body is the unconscious mind.
—CANDACE PERT

Being stuck in the mind is often reflected in the body as a feeling of congestion or being tightly held. If you simply observe people walking and talking you can get a sense of their internal state. Notice their sense of openness, friendliness, symmetry, and ease of motion, along with the tone, quality, and range of voice. Does the voice feel full, or does it feel shallow and pale or have a whining quality to it? Do the shoulders look rigid, the chest collapsed, the jaws tight? Or is there a sense of vitality, ease, and flow of motion? Do the words match the message? For example, if someone says, "I'd like to spend time with you," how convinced do you feel? Do they sound enthusiastic or halfhearted and bland? Let yourself see what you see, feel what you feel. Now turn toward yourself and make the same observations. Notice your body when you walk: what feels loose, what feels labored and tight? Take some time to swing your arms, roll your shoulders, sway, or undulate. Does it feel natural or weird and unfamiliar? As you go through your day, notice when you have fluttering in your stomach or tension in your jaw or any place that's tight. Also notice times when you feel relaxed and at ease in your body.

The body is like the weather—it changes, and responds to various internal and external conditions. Sometimes we have a chronic holding pattern; other times pangs of fear or apprehension arise in response to certain situations. We can use these reactions to either consider our response or ask ourselves, "What's this all about?"

Body awareness can help you to be aware of both physical and emotional stuck places. For example, fear might be signalled by a jagged burning sensation in the chest. Anger might be signalled by shutting down, having a tight jaw and fist, or turning to confusion and fear. For some anger leads to attacking, for still others it leads to self harm.

Peter Levine, in his excellent audiotapes on trauma (available from Sounds True) and his book *Waking the Tiger,* suggests that holding places in the body come from a response to fear or trauma in which an arousal pattern is evoked but not completed. For example, someone hurts you, and to shout back or run would be to risk greater violence. So you hold back. Thus, the physical fight-flight arousal patterns that were stimulated—adrenaline pumping, increased heart rate, cortisol, muscles tensing—never get discharged and remain stuck in your body. If you had been able to move, shake, or run—as animals do—the arousal cycle would have been completed and your body would have come to rest. These thwarted situations, whether they involve expressing grief or anger or standing up for yourself, lead to holding patterns in the body that can become chronic over time. That's why we hear the expression that anger, sadness, or other emotions are held in the body.

Think about the emotions you are often afraid to express and be aware of your body's physical response. I asked a client who had fallen into depression and was feeling listless and upset with her job to stand up and push back against my hands and think about who she was mad at. Suddenly her anger at her boss came blasting out, full throttle. "How dare you keep asking me to do more work! We're already at the breaking point. Do you have any idea of how much we already do? Back off! . . . You might even say thanks for a change." It was as if there were electrical circuits in her body that got hooked up and charged. Her eyes brightened, she laughed, and she felt better than she had in weeks. Instead of holding back, contracting, and getting depressed, her body and voice were in sync with her emotions and feelings. We could then talk about appropriate ways to talk to her boss.

Repressing or disowning our emotions extracts a terrible toll on our being—a kind of permanent imploding or contraction that can lead to feelings of exhaustion, anxiety, or depression. While we need to be appropriate in work situations or with family and friends, we can always let ourselves know how we feel along with the unedited version of what we'd like to say or do. We can practice letting our bodies move and feel. As a result, we can handle a situation more easily, with respect and good timing because we're no longer sitting on a volcano of emotion.

It's important to note that as we're expressing ourselves we need to get to the core emotions, not just spin on the surface. Some people complain or scream to cover up feelings of anger or shame or sadness. Others cry and appear helpless instead of expressing anger. What helps us to get unstuck is dropping down and connecting with our core feelings.

Becoming unstuck is about moving from constriction and frustration to flow, vitality, and ease. It's about an internal stability that allows you to experience calm amid the storm, accept the "what is" of life so you're not fighting against yourself. It's about having the courage to make major changes without losing sight of the little things you can do each day to soothe, delight, and bring you home to yourself.

Some questions to ponder:

- Do you feel shut off from your emotions and detached from your body, as if you're not really in it? Do conversations and situations seem almost unreal, as if you're looking at life through a Plexiglas wall? What sensations and emotions would arise if you came back into your body? Just ask yourself the question and see if anything arises. Don't work at it or "think" about it.

- Do you lack access to a wide range of human emotions? For example, you might be able to feel anger but not sadness, or sadness but not anger.

- Do you have chronic aches and pains with no perceivable source?

- Can you notice a connection between holding back emotions such as sadness, hurt, or fear, and what happens in your body or energy level as a result?

EXERCISE:

Tuning In to Your Body

1. Take a trip through your body. As if there's a little you with a flashlight, go through your whole body, noticing any tension, congestion, or pain, as well as places that are more relaxed. Whenever you come to a tense or blocked up part, take some time to focus on it, breathe into it, and simply be with it.

2. Notice the physical experience you have in response to the following: fear, anxiety, worry, sadness, loneliness, lack of assertiveness, as well as happiness, joy, feeling cared about. Do any of them reflect places where you feel stuck?

3. Stuck and Unstuck Thinking: What's the Difference?

> *Understanding is like water flowing in a stream. . . . In Buddhism knowledge is regarded as an obstacle for understanding. If we take something to be the truth, we may cling to it so much that even if the truth comes and knocks at our door, we won't want to let it in. . . . We must learn to transcend our own views*
>
> —THICH NHAT HANH, *THE HEART OF UNDERSTANDING*

There is a huge variation in the degree to which people get stuck. Everyone meets adversity in life, but even with difficult childhoods, economic strain, illness, divorce, insecurity, and boring jobs, some people rarely stay stuck for long. They hit bumps in the road, pick themselves up, regroup, and keep going. The predominant difference lies in an abiding faith in their ability to get through hard times, which includes resourcefulness, creativity, perseverance, taking action, and an ability to ask for help and cooperate with others.

Here is a scenario that demonstrates the difference between those who stay in the flow of life and those who get stuck: Imagine the unstuck people are driving down a bumpy, remote road in winter and the car breaks down after hitting a pothole. Within a short time they have built a lean-to from branches in the woods to keep them warm, someone has pooled all the food they had to share, and they then start a fire. Having taken care of their immediate needs, they sit in a circle to hear each other's ideas on what they should do to get help or who should start making the long trek to find someone. There is a sense of being in this predicament together, and they trust they will find a way.

The stuck people's car breaks down on a similarly remote road and the first reaction is panic and anger. "Oh God, this is terrible, what a stupid thing, we never should have come here." Harsh words follow: "You never should have hit that pothole," rebutted with, "I couldn't help it, everyone was talking so much I couldn't concentrate."

Tempers fray, tears of desperation fall, and a feeling of helplessness pervades. The remaining twelve-pack of beer is readily consumed and emotions become volatile. Without talking things over, someone leaves to walk fifteen miles to get help, which leaves others worried and upset. They sit in the car for a while and then get out and stand around. Each person feels alone with their fear and worried about what will happen. Any suggestion about what to do is countered with arguments of why it won't work.

Eventually both groups are rescued and taken to safety. The unstuck group will recall the experience as an adventure, feel close to each other, and have a deeper sense of their ability to master difficult situations. The stuck group will feel upset whenever they think about the experience, recall it as traumatic, and continue to feel strained in their relationships to each other. They have a deeper sense of fear about adventure and may curtail future explorations of this sort.

Building on these examples, here are some traits of people who live in a stuck mentality. In the following chapter I'll describe the qualities of those who generally stay unstuck.

Traits of People Who Are Stuck

Most of us have aspects of being stuck and unstuck. In general, the feeling of being stuck in life is the result of a whole constellation of factors, not just one. You can't necessarily measure being stuck by the outward appearance of one's actions. It's often the inner experience that determines whether a person is stuck. For example, one person might work relentlessly in a joyless pursuit to prove he is worthwhile or successful, while another person's hard work might stem from fascination, joy, and dedication. One will feel stressed, the other won't.

The descriptions that follow are tendencies and leanings rather than absolutes. For most people some fit and others don't. We'll start with the qualities of being stuck and then we'll look at the opposite qualities.

What Keeps People Stuck

1. *A sense of helplessness or lack of entitlement at one's core.* People who stay stuck have difficulty mobilizing themselves to take action. It's as if the will that leads to action has been thwarted or undeveloped. Opportunities come and go, but you remain on the outside looking in, feeling powerless to take a first step. Those better jobs or relationships are for other people. This doesn't mean that people who feel helpless or unentitled don't work hard. In fact, they often work very hard at unrewarding or unpleasant jobs. It's when they could improve their lives by stretching their minds, learning a new skill, or taking on a challenge that they become afraid or feel inertia overtake them.

2. *Negative thinking.* As a social worker friend who works with troubled families says, "No excuse is too small." When contemplating change, the mind immediately goes to something negative—why it won't work, how hard it is, how it hasn't worked in the past. It's either too difficult, too hot, too embarrassing, the wrong time of year, doesn't feel good, there isn't money, it would be awkward. People avoid doing anything that's the least bit uncomfortable rather than take action in their behalf.

3. *Keeping life chaotic.* People who stay stuck often have a chaotic approach to problem solving, planning, and organizing their lives. Impulsivity and emotion take over, while reason and planning get abandoned. They often get distracted and discouraged, fail to finish tasks, stick to a plan, or budget money for basics. When life

is chaotic, it lacks focus and often moves from one calamity to another. Bills are overdue, the leaking faucet becomes a flood, the weird sound in the car becomes an accident or a very expensive repair.

4. *An inability to calm or soothe oneself in healthy ways.* Some people stay in a revved up, agitated state because they lack healthy resources for calming themselves in the face of stress. Instead of breathing deeply, asking for support, or taking a break, they might resort to compulsive eating, addictions, sugar, stimulants, drugs, compulsive behavior, or ruminating for hours over a problem. From this state of unease, it's extremely difficult to relax or quiet the mind, so there is little room for being creative, making reasoned decisions, or feeling delight and happiness.

5. *Difficulty connecting with other people and a lack of a support system.* People who stay stuck often isolate themselves or feel highly anxious around others. They may fear being shamed, put down, left, or criticized. Without caring human connections we miss out on the support, spark of ideas, inspiration, encouragement, and friendship that can help motivate us to take a risk, look within, or solve problems.

6. *Looking to external sources for a sense of happiness or to feel "worthwhile."* People who get stuck often adopt the mistaken belief that status, possessions, looks, achievements, or success will prove that they are worthwhile or lovable. They may seek to anchor themselves with fame, money, sex, gurus, teachers, advisers, theories, belief systems, spiritual practices, images, or religion. But there are no magical answers to the need for acceptance of life as it is, with all its losses, turbulence, and beauty. While it's fine to read books and consult with teachers, in the end we need to quiet the mind, center ourselves, and be at peace with whatever is going on inside.

7. *Lack of an adequate concept of self-care and setting limits.* Self-care includes everything from getting enough sleep to eating well, exercising, getting physical checkups, saying what's true for you, making your dwelling place pleasant, keeping yourself from getting overly stressed, to having fun, exploring your talents, and feeling you have the right to live your own life. It means the ability to say No, Yes, and Maybe, without guilt or fear. Self-care is like breathing deeply, attuning to yourself, and treasuring the life you've been given. It's about balance, resonance, and taking appropriate action.

8. *A sense of self that is identified with images, concepts, and beliefs.* People get stuck because they equate their thoughts, beliefs, and ideas with their identity. They have an image of how they want to appear instead of finding out who they really are. They believe in absolute definitions of good, bad, right, and wrong, and are unable to see these as concepts and ideas with different possible interpretations.

9. *Repeating the same behavior and hoping the outcome will be different.* This can mean nagging your partner, lecturing your children, running your business in a certain way, overeating, avoiding problems, being unhealthy, or being overly tired. People who stay stuck just keep doing the same old thing, hoping by magic there will be a new result, but it rarely happens.

10. *Focusing on the overwhelming, how bad life is, and the terrible state of the world.* Many people in difficult situations continually focus on how overwhelmed, upset, and unhappy they feel. They talk about it, bond with others over their plight, get sympathy, and keep their minds on their problems. A variation on this theme is when people don't reveal themselves and instead talk about the terrible state of the world and all the stupid people who are running things. This keeps the downward spiral spinning, as opposed to

asking oneself, "What is one thing I can do today to make myself feel better? How can I be more personal in my relationships? How can I have a positive impact on the people or world around me?"

What's crucial to understand is how all these traits affect the nervous system and ability to relax and be in "wise mind." In other words, when we have an agitated, revved up mind or live in an exhausted body it's difficult to reason, be responsive, or make wise decisions. We tend to act on impulse or make survival decisions that preclude planning or thinking through the long-term consequences of our actions.

4. Traits of People Who Stay Unstuck . . . At Least Most of the Time

People who generally stay unstuck have a positive outlook, a way of reacting, and a set of beliefs that helps them regroup and keep going no matter what. It doesn't mean that they don't get stuck momentarily or face hardships or disappointment; it's that they have ways to fish themselves out and tread on. In reading through the qualities that follow, think about which traits seem most attainable and would be a good place to start.

1. *Confident in one's capacity to problem-solve and take action.* People who routinely move through life's challenges learn to take action when they start to feel stuck. They focus on all possibilities, explore numerous resources, are willing to try many solutions, and are open to creative approaches to the difficulties of life. They have the basic belief of "Where there's a will, there's a way." They take a problem-solving approach. And if one thing doesn't work, they try something else.

2. *Unwilling to remain in extremely unhappy or stressful situations indefinitely.* People who stay unstuck have a kind of happiness set point that is higher than people who stay stuck. They aren't willing to be sick and depressed indefinitely without doing something to try to remedy the situation. They believe life is too precious to be miserable and, bolstered by an inner confidence, they move to take action and effect change. They know that joy is possible—they've lived it and felt it—and it's where they want to be. Thus, when situations lead to stress, agitation, or pain, they look for ways to resolve, alter, or leave the situation.

3. *Able to give and receive support from friends and family.* People who stay unstuck are usually embedded in a community of friends, family, and/or a spiritual community. They can reach out for comfort, celebrate their joys, reveal their fears, trusting they will be accepted, and understood. These connections are deeply soothing and ease anxiety and feelings of alienation or separation.

4. *Do not attach their identity or ego to success or failure.* Life is experienced as an adventure with many parts—friendships, relationships, work, career, family, developing talents, and community. People who stay unstuck relish life and don't depend on achievement or accolades for a sense of self-worth. They might enjoy success, but the real joy is in the adventure—learning, creating, knowing, growing, having new experiences. They develop their gifts and talents but know they are not of their creation. They accept that you win some, lose some, and while they may feel sad or upset, they don't berate themselves when relationships or situations don't work out. They are more likely to experience their feelings, ask what they can learn from an experience, and then move on.

5. *Willing to experiment, try new ways of doing things, make mistakes, and then try again with a new plan.* Unstuck people aren't afraid of making mistakes in the interest of achieving a goal. If one approach

doesn't work, they try something different. Like children playing in a sandbox, spending hours making a castle, they are not hampered by endless thoughts of being right or wrong, of succeeding or failing; rather, they have visions, plans, or ideas and keep moving toward them. They might get mad, upset, or frustrated, but they can cool down and try again.

6. *Able to tolerate frustration and uneasiness in the interest of taking on a challenge.* Unstuck people are willing to be uncomfortable, uneasy, or to stretch their limits when it's required for a new adventure or in the interest of improving their life. They keep their focus on the big picture. For example, a person who is determined to have a more secure financial future takes control of his or her spending, perseveres through school or training, or takes a risk to move to a more favorable situation.

7. *Possess a sense of humor and lightheartedness.* Unstuck people generally see themselves as part of a greater flow of life and energy. As a result it becomes easier to relax, smile at their foibles, and have mercy on themselves and others when they make the same old mistake or have a hard time in a relationship. This broad perspective takes people from self-absorption to a kind of amused quality about themselves and the inevitable mistakes we all make. In turn they are more able to joke about themselves with others because there is no shame about their imperfections.

8. *Demonstrate profound care and concern for the well-being of all life.* Over and over I see that people who are generally unstuck see themselves as part of a larger community. They do not shield themselves from the suffering of others near and far and they participate in alleviating suffering, bringing kindness to others, and creating a more just world. This reflects their broad view of life and ability to get beyond self-absorption.

As you read this list, notice your reactions, both physical and mental. Do you pick up on how this list is lighter and more relaxed than the list of ways people keep themselves stuck?

As a psychotherapist working in the fields of trauma, addiction, and relationships for the past twenty-eight years, I am fully aware that many of the symptoms of being stuck stem from trauma. But painful experiences are not a life sentence. Many people have shifted from operating primarily in a stuck way to living more in accord with the qualities of being unstuck.

As a starting place, be completely compassionate and merciful with yourself—accept wherever you are this moment. Recognizing how and where you're stuck is a crucial step to getting unstuck. It's also important not to focus on the stuck aspects of your life, but rather take whatever items on the unstuck list that seem within your grasp and start practicing them in the same way you'd learn a new skill.

EXERCISE:

Beginning Steps for Getting Unstuck

1. Notice whenever your mind goes to negative or helpless thinking, and say, "negative," or "oops." Then have a pithy direct phrase to shift your perspective. "Okay, now what can I do?" "There's got to be a way." "People have changed their situation, so can I." "What's one step I can take today?" Shifting to proactive thinking is like jump-starting your system.

2. Notice when you are operating out of an emotionally-charged mind. Notice when you bring reason and reality to your thinking. Notice when you think through the long-term effects or consequences of your behavior.

3. Bond in joy and power with people and avoid bonding in pain, helplessness, and misery. Resist endless negative talk inside your

head or with other people. Talk about what you are doing to take care of yourself, and take time to have fun with others.

5. Ease Your Way to Getting Unstuck with Buddhist Teachings

Zen in its essence is the art of seeing into the nature of one's own being, and it points the way from bondage to freedom.
—D. T. SUZUKI, *ESSAYS IN BUDDHISM*

Buddhism offers a gentle and wise understanding of being stuck and getting unstuck. The Buddha's focus was to explore the cause of suffering and the end of suffering. Once we understand that our misery is mostly self-created through our thoughts, attachments, or being controlled by sense desires, we have a powerful tool for moving out of our stuck places. We'll start with the teachings called the Four Noble Truths.

The Four Noble Truths

The First Noble Truth, or the Truth of Dukkha: *Life inevitably includes suffering or difficulty.* Life can be scary, insecure, and difficult. We all experience change, loss, disappointment, illness, and eventually death. It's the "what is" of life. When we fight against these events rather than being with them, we create an inner duality that leads to tension and suffering. In the Buddha's day, *dukkha* referred to wheels with axles that were off center or bones that had slipped out of their sockets. Thus "the truth of *dukkha*" implies that we live life off center, out of joint, or out of sync when we resist our experience by blaming or saying it's unfair or shouldn't have happened.

The Second Noble Truth: Life is painful or difficult because of our attachments. You suffer when you demand that life be different than it is or when you are dragged around by sense cravings. When you accept that life is challenging and difficult your suffering eases. People who live with continuous "shoulds" in their minds are ignoring the "what is" of life, namely that bosses make too many demands, babies cry, we make mistakes, it rains on the garden party, and people are capable of immense cruelty to each other, along with kindness and love.

It's our attachment to something being different rather than the situation itself that causes suffering. Imagine two people who both lose their jobs. One is rageful, can't sleep, is angry at the company, and feels worthless as a result of not having work. The other person, while not happy with the situation, looks around for volunteer work, considers downsizing his lifestyle, and starts exploring all the possibilities. He is able to enjoy his free time and has no sense of failure because he doesn't equate having a job with who he is. Same situation, different reactions based on levels of attachment or non-attachment.

On the path of getting unstuck we become responsible for our own emotional turbulence.

As a starting place for recognizing attachments, simply notice your physical and emotional reactions when something doesn't go your way. If you get irritated, afraid, upset, or hurt, it signals that you are demanding that a person or situation be different than it is. It is your attachment that creates your suffering, not the actual event.

Any time you feel upset, angry, judgmental, hurt, and so on, if you'll notice your emotions (how you are suffering) and what you want to be different, you will tap into your ego-judging mind.

The concept of attachment also relates to your emotional experience. To push away natural expressions of grief, sorrow, anger, and hurt is to shut down against one's humanness, or you could say it becomes an attachment to not feeling. As a result, you become habituated to holding back, avoiding, or disowning parts of yourself, which creates holding patterns in the body. These manifest as repetitive responses to life situations—automatically becoming afraid, defensive, resisting change, or tightening up throughout the body. These patterns are conveyed through your body language, movement, and voice—there is an incongruence or sense of being off center. This leads to what Buddhism refers to as *samsara*—the wheel of suffering—having unconscious, repetitive emotional responses to life's situations . . . a.k.a. being stuck.

The Third Noble Truth: Ease and peace of mind are possible. The Third Noble Truth is the step of hope—there is a way out. Peace of mind is possible. If we allow ourselves to be exactly where we are in the moment—fully present, noticing whatever is happening inside us and outside us—we can trade in judgment, fear, and shame for curiosity and fascination. Through awareness we start easing our demands, expectations, rituals, and self-grasping. We go about our lives, give it our best, and let go of the outcome. Even if it's momentarily uncomfortable we learn to drop down into our body where we are closer to experience, thus our real self. We become more of an observer to life's dramas; we are no longer embroiled in them.

The Fourth Noble Truth: The path toward greater ease and peace is found in the Eightfold Path. The Buddha created eight steps to be used as a guide to living an enlightened life. This path encompasses the categories of wisdom (right view, right intentions), ethics (right speech, right action, right livelihood, right effort), and meditation (right mindfulness, right concentration). They are circular stepping stones to help lead us away from attachments and external trappings, into the heart of our existence. They are about living from a place of truth, mindfulness, understanding, and acceptance in all aspects of our lives.

Impermanence

If the Four Noble Truths help us to see how we create suffering by clinging to our thoughts, the concept of impermanence reminds us that nothing is static. Everything is dynamic, alive, interacting, and in motion—the cells, molecules, atmosphere, thoughts, plants, animals. You are a fluid process interchanging energy with everything around you—the air, water, food, people, weather, scenery, relationships. So when someone says, "That's just the way I am," it would be more accurate to add, "at this moment."

Thich Nhat Hanh writes in *The Diamond That Cuts Through Illusion*, "Words and concepts are rigid and motionless, but reality is a steadily flowing stream. It is impossible to contain a living reality in a rigid framework." Thus, to be alive is to drop whatever creates a rigid framework, and accept the ever-changing flow of life.

Form Is Emptiness, Emptiness Is Form

In Buddhism we learn to notice our attachments and our internal experience of breathing, tension, and relaxation, while we see how our lives are set against the backdrop of all creation, remembering that our thoughts, bodies, minds, objects, and air around us are all made of one energy. *Specifically, form is emptiness and emptiness is form.* Everything rises and falls from one source, one energy. This helps us remember that while we are studiously working to finish a project, arguing with our mate, or upset because we gained ten pounds, the earth continues to spin around the sun, gravity is keeping our feet on the ground, animals are hunting for food, rivers are running, clouds are gathering moisture, and people all over the world are having their own struggles, sometimes similar to ours, and often much more challenging, and it's all part of one energy.

Buddhism is about becoming one with the flow of life—we enter a river with its rocks and riffles, its boulders, log jams, and smooth waters. Sometimes we feel calm in the center of the storm: I remember when my sister was dying, she wanted none of our tears. She wanted us to laugh together, reveal our long-buried secrets, and have us circle her hospital bed singing, "You Are My Sunshine." Other times lightning strikes: we lose our grounding and feel shaken and changed. The God of our childhood collapses, our lover leaves, the work that sustained us no longer satisfies.

But from a bigger perspective, we remember it's all part of one journey—our personal journey and that of all people. Whatever we experience, others are cycling through the same emotions and struggles—albeit with different rhythms, settings, and costumes. As we will explore, peacefulness comes when we tap into the knowledge that we are all bound together by a field of consciousness that permeates everything.

Imagine the teachings of the Buddha like the ringing of a bell. Let them vibrate, touch you, or be a guide, but do not grab hold of them as the ultimate knowledge. It is often said that the teachings provide the raft to take you across the river, but as you land on the opposite shore the raft comes apart and you find yourself walking on your own— eyes and heart open—experiencing the immensity and wonder of life.

6. Am I Stuck or Am I Floundering: What's the Difference?

I recently spoke with my niece Alissa. "I'm really stuck," she said with a laugh. "I'm sick of teaching in a private high school for boys, but I don't know what else I want to do. I think of going back to school or changing jobs, but nothing excites me. I hear people who've had this job for twenty years making the same complaints I make after one year. I want to say, 'If you don't like it, do something different.' I don't want to be here in twenty years with the same complaints they have."

I laughed. "You're not stuck," I told her. "You're just floundering. You'd be stuck if you were rationalizing your unhappiness and saying there was nothing you could do. But you're out there looking and exploring, and most of all you believe it's possible to be happier." Alissa's willingness to know and feel her unhappiness and to be casting about for something better is a mark of unstuck thinking. She may not know what she wants—we often don't—but she knows this isn't it. That's the first step.

There is a paradox about attachment that often comes up in spiritual circles. One might say that Alissa is attached to her job being different. Does that mean she should try to dissolve her attachments and try to accept her job? Some people might say yes, but I disagree. I repeatedly see people getting sick and feeling miserable trying to tough it out with jobs and relationships that aren't working. *It's important to come into reality and say, "This isn't working, I'm not doing well, I need to leave."* The more we fight against these signals from inside the more we are likely to get sick or depressed.

Yes, we can try to adjust how we feel and make an effort to change our situation for the better, but if there comes a point when you wake up every day with a knot in your gut, you dread going to work, want to sleep or eat chocolate all day, or feel a scream deep inside you, it's time to hear the message—it's not working. Buddhism doesn't teach that you have to continue doing something you don't like. It's about listening to all the signals and realizing when it's time to move on.

A month later, Alissa told me triumphantly that she had quit her job and was applying for teaching positions in several locations, some far away. This typifies another trait of people who get unstuck. They are willing to make big changes without guarantees. Alissa figured she could do all kinds of jobs to get by if a teaching position didn't materialize.

A few days later, I spoke with Alissa's sister, Danielle, twenty-six, who excitedly told me she was leaving a high-paying job in New York City, which had once been her dream, to start a doctoral program in psychology. Then I heard that her brother Alex, who was a sophomore at Columbia University, had decided to switch universities because he wanted a different sort of music program. Finally, I heard that the third sister had just been accepted to a small Southern college. Four children, four different universities, four changes. Clearly, this is a family that encourages unstuck thinking when it comes to jobs and lifestyles.

Floundering is the space between letting go of one job and finding another, leaving one relationship and meeting new people. It's the dissonance before the resolution. The tension before the relaxation. It's a necessary part of change. It's our ability to tolerate this discomfort that helps us get unstuck because we don't make hasty decisions to quell our agitation. We ride it out and keep looking for a situation that is better.

The floundering times in our lives can be simultaneously uncomfortable and exciting. There's an anticipation of change mixed with a big question mark about what's coming. So much is open to us. We can talk with others, hear their stories, play with ideas, explore new possibilities, and then live with patience (or impatience) as our path unfolds. We can remember that in many ways we're following life as it comes to us. So remember, make your best effort, let go of the outcome, then relax and enjoy the passing show.

7. What Makes Change So Scary? Explore the Payoffs That Keep You Stuck

The human mind likes a strange idea as little as the body likes a strange protein and resists it with a similar energy.
—W. I. BEVERIDGE, SCIENTIST

Why is change so hard? Because we adopted most of our behaviors to survive or comfort ourselves in some way. Sneakiness, lying, compulsive eating, shutting down, thrill seeking, burying feelings, being perfect, or acting like a victim initially served a purpose. Namely they helped us get approval, attention, or sympathy, avoid being shamed, feel excitement, or escape feeling horrible about ourselves. Unfortunately, many of these behaviors became the escape hatches that now keep us stuck. They are the counterfeit comforts, the short-term forms of relief that block long-term happiness.

I went back and forth on whether to use the term payoffs because of its sinister connotation, as in one gets paid off for some kind of dirty deal or a sign of weakness. The psychological term, secondary gains, is indeed accurate and softer, but it sounds so technical. In this context I'm asking the question, "What do you get from a behavior that makes it hard to give up, even though it's hurting you in many ways?" The second question is, "What would help you give it up? Can you see how much it's hurting you, and what you have to gain?"

Long-standing payoffs for certain types of behavior can feel like good old friends. Giving up payoffs means eliciting the spiritual warrior within us. I don't believe anyone truly *wants* to be stuck or stay stuck. However, the gains or payoffs from stuck behavior can be a powerful force in keeping us stuck. For example, if I give up portraying myself as a pathetic victim, I will have to give up the sympathy I get from others. If I give up blaming the world (mother, father, horoscope, injustice) for my problems, I will have to take action on my own behalf . . . and I may not have a clue how to get started. This can feel daunting.

Admitting to the payoffs for hanging onto our our stuck places can be embarrassing—we hate to admit to the ways we elicit guilt, manipulate others to feel sorry for us, or avoid responsibility. *But remember, you need to acknowledge your payoffs if you want to get unstuck.* In past therapy groups we'd often have a session at which we would reveal how we conned or manipulated other people through our sad stories, guilt-inducing words, or intimidation. Everyone would usually start out feeling sheepish, but by the end we were laughing at ourselves and feeling an amazing amount of energy. This reflects how freeing it is to admit to our lies and cons. As one woman said, "It's kind of like, the game is up! I can't do that anymore and play innocent."

Remember, *the idea of exploring the payoffs from your stuck places is to bring them on screen and become aware of them so you have a choice about what you want to do—you can't let go of what you don't acknowledge.*

Payoff Inventory/Secondary Gains

The following list is inspired in part by Ken Keyes's *The Methods Work If You Do,* and in part by a list I created for my clients many years ago.

Read each question to yourself, or have someone read it to you. Notice your internal reactions—which ones elicit a response and which ones don't? Answer with just a few words or sentences, and notice when you start to rationalize, analyze, or make excuses . . . What's that about?

Bring up a habit or behavior that has you stuck and is hard to let go of, then see if any of the following items fit. (Examples: not speaking up, berating yourself, overworking, isolating.)

1. *I get to distract myself from underlying feelings of emptiness, loneliness, fear, and sadness with this behavior.* (Example: eating chocolate, staying busy, overworking, focusing on others, staying in a chaotic relationship.)

2. *This behavior is soothing and lowers my anxiety.* (Examples: compulsive sex, eating, cleaning, chocolate, working, being perfect, gossiping, isolating, not speaking up.)

3. *I get sympathy and attention.* (People feel sorry for me, worry about me, and call to help me. This feels as if I'm loved.)

4. *I get approval, admiration, status, rewards, money.* People want to be with me.

5. *I get a sense of intensity.* It's exciting and life feels important. I might feel depressed or bored without this intensity.

6. *I get to avoid revealing myself.* (Examples: one-upmanship, talking about other people, ranting about the terrible state of the world.)

7. *I get to avoid taking responsibility for the state of my life.* (Examples: blaming, talking about my terrible childhood.) Nothing is ever about my lack of effort or mistakes; it's always about other people or situations.

8. *I keep people from confronting me or being angry with me.* (Examples: I'm in such pain and my life is so difficult; I'm so sweet, generous, and innocent; I'm so intimidating.)

9. *I get to be right, and make others wrong.* I can feel superior, righteous, and above others, and I don't have to see their suffering.

10. *I get to fit in and not threaten anyone.* (Examples: rescuing others, being agreeable, not asking for anything, hiding my intelligence, opinions, and needs.)

11. *I get to have a sense of belonging.* (Examples: joining with people who also talk about their wounds, engage in addictions, or believe it's us against the world.)

12. *I get to avoid looking at my part in a troubled situation* by blaming and trying to get everyone else to change. I analyze others and tell stories about the crazy/mean things they do.

13. *I get to be a martyr and make other people feel guilty.* (Examples: I'm so good, I'm suffering so much, maybe they'll give me money, take care of me, and not ask anything of me in return.)

14. *I have an excuse for poor performance or not being responsible. People won't expect anything out of me.* (Examples: I'm in great distress, my life is such a mess.)

15. *I get to avoid making mistakes or feeling incompetent.* (Example: I don't stretch myself or try anything new.)

16. *I get to feel sorry for myself, or they'll feel sorry for what they did!* (Example: I dwell on my bad luck or tough life or get others to feel guilty.)

17. *I get to convince myself I'm doing something useful.* (Instead of facing reality and taking action I endlessly analyze my situation, talk with friends, see psychics, read books, get advice, see therapists, go to spiritual retreats. This also applies to endlessly processing painful relationships.)

18. *I get to avoid the terror of emptiness.* (Examples: staying busy at all times, talking compulsively, developing addictions, having life in chaos.)

19. *I never have to reach out to others. I get to remain invulnerable and not risk rejection by never asking for help or support.* (Examples: I isolate, avoid social situations, and keep distance from people.)

20. *I get to remain in a fantasy world.* (Instead of seeing the "what is" of my situation, I can fantasize about how it might have been. I can also stay in a state of euphoric recall about sex, food, romance, or getting an award, for example.)

21. *Other. Make up one of your own.*

EXERCISE:

What Would It Take to Make a Change?

1. Ask yourself, "How is this payoff behavior causing me to suffer?"

2. Ask yourself, "How could I get what I want without using this payoff behavior," e.g., "How could I calm myself, get comfort, ease my pain, or connect with people without a harmful behavior?" Give a lot of attention to this question. We don't usually let go of a soothing behavior without having a new one available to us.

3. Consciously practice your payoff behavior. You might even exaggerate it. Be aware of your body sensations, energy level, and emotions. Then, in another situation, resist doing it and see how you feel.

4. If you feel anxious, empty, or uneasy when you don't act out your payoff behavior, sit with the feelings without either expressing or repressing them. The more you raise your capacity to handle feelings and contain them, the less you will need your payoff behavior.

5. Ask yourself, "What beliefs about myself keep this payoff behavior going?" For example, it's no big deal, I'll quit tomorrow, just this once.

6. Talk with someone about your payoff behavior and tell them you want to make a change. Ask if you could call them to check in about how it's going.

7. If it feels too hard to do on your own, find a skilled therapist to help you. Sometimes there is a lot of underlying pain and trauma, and we need a supportive person to be with us when we face strong feelings.

8. Remember, once again, we let go of a payoff behavior because it causes us to suffer in the long run, and keeps us from feeling at one with ourselves. It's not about fixing yourself or being better or worse—Buddhism does not attach judgments to what you do, rather, it focuses on degrees of being conscious and unconscious, awake or asleep. You can let go or not let go, and in the cosmic scheme of things it's still all One Energy. So be easy with yourself either way.

8. Step Beyond Your Fears

For a mind burdened with fear, with conformity, with the thinker, there can be no understanding of that which may be called the original.

—J. KRISHNAMURTI, *On Fear*

Fear is like a shadowy force hiding under our excuses, criticism, need to control, worry, and feelings of emptiness. Whenever you hear yourself making excuses, being evasive, or trying to control a person or situation, ask yourself, "What am I afraid of?" Stay with this question and peel down through the surface layers, even though your ego self may want to resist. Then drop all the words, and allow the fear to exist against a background of stillness until you actually feel it as a physical sensation in your body. The idea is not to escape, push away, or abolish fear; rather, it is to be aware of its existence. This presents a paradox: while we want to have less fear, the approach is not to get rid of it or push it away because that only creates inner warfare. The first step is to acknowledge its presence.

Many of our daily fears are based on *anticipating* shame, hurt, uneasiness, emptiness, sadness, or grief that *might* occur. We fear feelings that *might* arise, depending on our interpretation of an event. For example, I might say I'm afraid to go back to school because I *might* not do well, *and* then believe I'm unworthy. I create a story that gets me agitated or afraid. *If there's no story, there's no fear.*

We need to remember that it's words, concepts, and beliefs that often keep us afraid. *Telling ourselves* we're inadequate can lead to dreaded feelings of shame and guilt. If we didn't have those concepts and ideas in our minds, experiences would not hold the risk of so-called failure. Mary's story went like this: "I got back an English paper with generally positive responses, but on one page there was the comment, 'this is a bit of a cliché.' My mind started down the track of, 'I'm a failure, I can't write, I might as well give up, why did I come to graduate school anyhow. I might as well quit and kill myself.'" She laughed, then continued: "The next day when I was calm, I looked over the paper again and was able to see all the positive remarks. When I got to the cliché remark, I realized it was true and not a big deal. I keep wondering how did I get so totally messed up by that one remark?"

Fear is also biological. It is a hardwired reaction to *perceived* danger and often manifests itself by momentary freezing or feeling stunned. That's what triggered Mary's reaction. Because fear so automatically arises out of the past, we forget that it is a conditioned reaction. Fear usually means that a childlike part of us is perceiving the situation.

Adults with a history of childhood trauma or attachment injuries often have automatic fear reactions, particularly in close relationships. This could include worries such as, "What will people think of me?" "Am I doing it right?" "What will happen if I'm alone?" You can ask this question: "Which part of me is feeling the fear?" When I help clients to delve into their fears, we often discover a tiny child part of themselves whose very survival feels at stake. A terror of non-existence comes up that began years ago because no one responded adequately to their basic need for touch, food, comfort, and connection. As a child, this fear made biological sense because the child was dependent on the parent. As an adult, however, it is not rational from a survival perspective because we can now take care of ourselves.

If someone being late or saying no to you rekindles these dreaded childhood feelings, you can elicit your adult self to observe and handle the situation. There are two things you can do. First, look inside to the part of you that is afraid, look him or her in the eyes, notice how old he or she is, pick up that child part and hold him or her internally and give comfort. Second, bring the situation into current reality by saying to the child part, "I understand why you were scared as a child, but it's now the year ____. I'm __ years old and I can dress myself, feed myself, walk, go potty, buy food, earn money, and take care of my basic needs." This is necessary because the child part got frozen in time and is reacting on automatic without knowledge that time has passed.

It's like helping a child at night who is afraid of dragons in the closet. You kindly go in, open the closet door, and turn on the light of current time. "See—let's take a look behind the clothes, on the shelf. Come on, let's look together." You help the child sort out fact from fiction. If you make it a habit to "turn on the light of reality" and go no further with your mind, fear subsides on its own.

Fear can also relate to repressing our biological animal self. We have been taught to fear that which is wild, hungry, passionate, sexy, raucous, and cover it with a polite exterior. We try to contain it, squash it, get rid of it as if somehow it is unholy or dangerous. This leads to getting stuck at a very basic level because we are afraid of that which is human/animal within us. When we delve into the wholeness of our being, and truly make friends with creation as expressed through our bodies, we live in the flow of life rather than in fear.

Krishnamurti makes the crucial connections between absence of fear, moving beyond obedience, and realizing our mind is part of the total mind: "When the human mind is free of all fear, then in demanding to know what the original is, it is not seeking its own pleasure, or means of escape, and therefore in that inquiry all authority ceases. . . . The authority of the speaker, the authority of the church, the authority of opinion, of knowledge, of experience, of what people say—all that completely comes to an end, and there is no obedience. It is only such a mind that can find out for itself what the original is—find out, not as an individual mind, but as a total human being— the total mind."

In relation to getting unstuck, we need to explore how fear often stops forward motion or taking the next step. "Oh, I can't do that, I'm afraid." That's where we need to bring our concerns into current reality—is there really any serious danger of starving, dying, or being injured?—if not we need to take the next step, fear and all. To move with life is to penetrate these fears, observe them, and step through them. Usually nothing terrible happens no matter what the outcome.

When exploring your fears, it's important to realize there is a natural uneasiness or apprehension most people feel when faced with a challenge or trying something new. That is different from being controlled by childhood fears that are not valid in current time and block us from taking steps to get unstuck in life.

EXERCISE:

Moving Through Fear

1. Think of a time you were afraid but you took action anyhow, and the outcome was positive or nothing terrible happened. How did you get yourself to move beyond your fear? What did you say to

yourself? Take time to plant this in your memory bank so you can call on this memory when you feel afraid.

2. Take something you are afraid of doing and ask yourself, "What's the worst thing that could happen?" For example, in deciding to have a heart-to-heart talk with a special friend, you may meet the fear that she won't be your friend anymore. So ask, Then what? I'll feel sad. Then what? I'll try to talk with her. Then what? If it doesn't work out, I'll at least feel that I tried. Then what? I'll go to other friends, but I'll still miss her. Then what? I'll be sad, but I'll be okay.

3. Make a clear agreement with some friends that you can call them in time of need. Marcie was going through a very hard time after her daughter moved away and her job was in jeopardy. "Sometimes I'd start pacing around the house like an animal going crazy. I finally mustered the strength to ask a friend at work if I could call her when I was freaking out at home. When she said she'd be honored if I called her, I was moved to tears. Just knowing she was there gave me great comfort."

STEP TWO

Show Up

Show Up

9. The Buddha Is Everywhere, Waiting to Guide You

Who is wise? He who learns from all men.
—TALMUD

Everything is Buddha energy—all people, all life, all feelings, all things. There is no separate Buddha, there is simply a process of waking up.

We now take a second step and move from reflection on our stuck places to motion. Without necessarily knowing what we want to change (other than we want something different) or where we'll end up, we open ourselves to life's experiences and tune in to messages we get from people, books, situations, events, and stillness. To show up is to meet life with fascination and curiosity rather than fear, worry, and foreboding. And if there is fear, you can show up anyhow.

Messages come from surprising places—in the form of the person sitting next to you on a bus, from a dance lesson, going to a movie, or wandering through a bookstore—you never know when it will come. The guidance, inspiration, and connecting links we need can be found all around you if you only stop to tune in.

If you've ever watched toddlers at play, you'll notice they move around touching, tasting, feeling, and bringing fascination to whatever is around—from scraps of paper, to pillows, to measuring cups, to the cat. They pick up a block, look at it, lick it, put it in a pile with other blocks, then move on to something else. They aren't saying, "Now I'll pick up a block, now I'll set it down"; they are pulled by all their senses to explore smells, sights, textures, tastes, and tones. They are led by fascination and curiosity. That is the essence of deciding where you want to show up. You are guided by a deep sense of resonance with yourself. What calls you, stirs you to excitement, and touches on your life's desires? This doesn't mean anything goes. From a Buddhist perspective, we always consider what we do in the context of integrity and a commitment to kindness, honesty, and doing no harm to ourselves and others.

To show up is to put yourself into a web of connections that can broaden your perspective, give you fresh ideas, and open possibilities you never even dreamed of. Consider the story of Elaine, who took her first flying lesson at the age of forty, after leaving a seasonal job in Antarctica. Usually quiet and withdrawn, Elaine felt a sense of elation from soaring high in the sky, learning about the weather patterns, and mastering something that had always intrigued her. She had tiny glimpses of what it might be like to become a pilot, but because she didn't believe it was possible, lacked money, and was afraid she wouldn't get hired anywhere, she dropped the idea. She subsequently became depressed trying to figure out what to do.

Then, several months later, Elaine was at a workshop on healing with her friend, Sophia. Sophia struck up a lunchtime conversation with a man named Mike, who happened to be a pilot. "What's the situation like for women now?" Sophia asked, smiling back at Elaine.

"It's great," he said. "The airlines are really wanting to hire more women pilots."

"What does it cost? Is it really expensive?"

"Yes," he replied, "but there are all kinds of scholarships and loans you can take out."

"Do you think it's too late at forty to get started?"

"Not at all!"

Elaine's ears had perked up by then. The next day Mike casually dropped a flying magazine on Elaine's lunch table. It included ads and descriptions of the various flying schools in the country.

Elaine is now a pilot. Although the job climate changed dramatically after 9/11, just when she had been offered a contract with a commercial airline, Elaine found a niche in teaching. But if she hadn't been with Sophia or shown up at the healing conference, she wouldn't have gotten started. Mike and Sophia were the links to her new career, but it was Elaine who picked up the catalogue and took it from there.

Showing up might be as simple as pulling yourself out of bed and taking a little walk when you feel sad or depressed. Here is the raspberry story: Jeanette was feeling achy, exhausted, and depressed several days after major surgery. She couldn't seem to pull herself out of bed or make an effort to do anything. After several days, with her husband's encouragement, and struggling against a desire to roll over and go back to sleep, she dragged herself out of bed and wandered into the backyard. "It was rather bleak and colorless," she told me. "All the flowers were faded, the leaves had fallen, and the sky was was gray. I walked around looking at the silhouettes of the bushes, feeling the leaves crunch under my feet, and suddenly, my eye caught one bright red raspberry hanging on a bush. I marvelled at how it came to be ripe at this time when all the other berries were gone. I thought about all the forces of nature that brought forth this lone little raspberry that seemed so cheerful and alive. I picked the raspberry and popped it in my mouth. The sweet taste awakened me as if life was pouring into me again." Her depression lifted almost completely and she stayed up most of the day, looking out the window, taking care of things around the house, and calling a neighbor. "I often think of that little berry," she said, "and wonder how could it have made so much of a difference."

How can a sweet little raspberry have so much power to transform our lives? A tiny experience can open us to an amazing flow of energy. It's like finding the core switch and giving it a gentle tap so it can feed into every part of the body and spirit.

10. Feel the Exquisite Dance of Mind, Body, and Spirit

Every time we are touched, experience awe, feel treasured by another person, or have our minds and hearts stimulated, we are setting off the complex biochemical system in the body that leads to a sense of well-being. Likewise, we can give the same to others. The power of a welcoming smile, hug, or help when we need it is a reminder of the power we have when we show up for each other. It's as if we become the ripe raspberry, a bit of sweetness in one another's lives.

There is nothing separate in the body-mind complex. We are an intricate interwoven network of many systems and receptors, all affecting and interacting with each other. Candace Pert, in her compelling book *Molecules of Emotion*, poses the question, "How can emotions transform the body, either creating disease or healing it, maintaining health or undermining it?" In her research spanning three decades she has come to see that, "When there is a flow of chemical information that is unimpeded, it results in homeostasis, or balance." Furthermore, the ability to express emotions instead of keeping them blocked up is the key to creating that flow. If we are holding back our sadness, hurt, anger, or joy, we block the flow in the body, thus compromising the immune system and our mental outlook. Pert also writes, "I believe that happiness is what we feel when our biochemicals of emotion, the neuropeptides and their receptors, are open and flowing freely throughout the psychosomatic network, integrating and coordinating our systems, organs, and cells in a smooth and rhythmic movement."

And this is not done with medications and drugs; it happens through the free flow of feelings and emotions, a flow which is deeply linked to being connected in the world—to people, nature, and the ability to feel love and awe.

This process underscores one of the deepest reasons for showing up in life. The inner flow of our emotional and biochemical network is tremendously related to the flow of our connection to nature, beauty, experience, and supportive connections with other people. Reconnecting with an old friend, learning a new skill, focusing on being true to ourselves, helping plant a community garden, or cooking a lovely dinner with a friend all wake up parts of us and increase this inner flow, thus feeding into our emotional well-being.

Showing up is not always about getting out and doing something; it's more about showing up for what you need in your life, which could mean to take time for stillness, a relaxed meal with a friend, reflection, journaling, or meditation. It might mean doing less of what drains you and more of what feeds your life.

EXERCISE:

Feeling the Flow Within You

1. Think back on a time when something small—a kind word, gesture, taste, touch, view, song, or chance meeting brought you out of a dreary place. Remember the shift you felt and notice what happens in your body as you remember this.

2. What would bring you a measure of delight today? What one small thing? Repeat this exercise every day for a week, then for two weeks.

3. Take a conscious walk. Focus on the rhythm and movement of your body and how your feet connect with the ground. Notice what flows easily and what feels impeded.

11. Show Up Just the Way You Are Right Now

Most of us go to our graves with our music still inside us.
—OLIVER WENDELL HOLMES

Many people say they need to be different than they are before they can shift their lives. I disagree. *Now* is a great time to show up for something new. Don't wait to play the music within you; don't let the instrument get out of tune or fall apart.

You create self-acceptance by showing up just the way you are right now! *That means you can show up:*

interested	unprepared
afraid	ashamed
worried	confused
overweight	depressed
tired	with opinions
curious	with a blank mind
preoccupied	with expectations
with thinning hair	with anger
anxious	with love
happy	and many other combinations of
sad	qualities and feelings
messed up	

What is something you've wanted to do, but never got around to? Piano lessons, flying, aikido, calling on a neighbor, trying out for a play, painting the bathroom purple? Take those thoughts out of the recesses of your mind and bring them into the foreground. Why not? Why not do it soon? It doesn't matter how you do it. What do you have to lose? To the extent you are willing to do it for the fun or adventure of it, it's less likely to provoke anxiety.

You don't have to be totally confident, fearless, or clear. Life sometimes is uncertain, blurry, and confusing, and you can still take action.

Another way to show up is to tell someone you messed up a job, or that you feel lost or clumsy, or that you did something quite brilliant. Take whatever you tend to hide out of the closet and let it be known. To paraphrase the song, "Self-acceptance is another word for nothing left to hide." Every time you reveal yourself there's more flow on the inside, and there's less to hide or be afraid of. Many people don't talk to others about themselves because they don't feel worthy of being listened to or they feel ashamed of their actions or problems. Acceptance requires that we break such patterns.

Showing up just the way you are helps you relax into your natural self. We're not here to put on masks; we're here to live, explore, learn, and feel joy.

To show up for life feeling awkward or afraid is more expansive than to appear with a cheerful mask that hides your feelings. At the heart of acceptance you can remember the Buddhist teaching that everything is One Energy; nothing is inherently bad about singing off-key, being afraid, or doing a mediocre job, just as there is nothing inherently good about joy and happiness, or getting a positive evaluation. *There is our momentary experience—and when we deny it, we deny ourselves.*

So take your perfectly imperfect self and show up for something new, be it a conversation, a class, or a quiet hour. Showing up for a new experience will be easy or difficult; you'll enjoy it or you won't; it will lead you where you want to end up, or it won't. It's all part of the same dance. Just do it and see what happens.

12. Learn to Step Out of Your Own Way

> *At the historic core of every religion is not ritual, but someone
> who broke through ritual to direct contact with the transcendental.
> They were discovering it and living it. Moses, Jesus, Buddha, Lao-
> tzu, Mohammed were not following anything but the expression of
> their direct contact with the actuality of life.*
>
> —STEVEN HARRISON, *DOING NOTHING*

Years ago, in a state of rapture at a concert by flautist Jean-Pierre Rampal, my friend Martha Boesing leaned over and said, "It's so beautiful. It's as if he gets out of the way and lets the music come through him."

I've pondered for years what it means to get out of the way of what I'm doing. For starters I've wondered, who's getting out of the way of whom? It seems there are two parts within each person: one part that plays the instrument and the other part—the ego—that needs to get out of the way. What I've come to understand is this: there is the spirit of me—a spirit in a body, a conduit of energy, all the knowledge, muscle memory, and experience of my lifetime. And then there is the conditioned ego of me—the voices ready to jump in with thoughts of good, bad, beautiful, or ugly. Just as Rampal let his ego fall away so he was a conduit for the music, when we let our conditioned ego fall away we dwell in experience and connect with the essence of life.

Getting out of the way of oneself is similar to what athletes, musicians, and other creative people often call "being in the zone." There's no beginning, no ending, no going anywhere. Essentially, it means you're not thinking, judging, or critiquing what's going on; your body is in the flow of the experience and you are responding and reacting based on everything you know, without having to think about it. Thoughts come to you, but without agitation or worry, as if you are not the thinker.

What does this have to do with showing up? It takes us to the question of who is showing up, your ego or your spirit? Shunryu Suzuki, in *Zen Mind, Beginner's Mind*, addressed this question in talking about meditation:

> The most important thing is to forget all gaining ideas, all dualistic ideas. Do not think about anything. Just remain on your cushion without expecting anything. Then eventually you will resume your own true nature. That is to say, your own true nature resumes itself.

Ponder the words, "your own true nature resumes itself." You don't *make* your true nature happen, you step out of the way and feel its presence. It's always there, like the sun behind the clouds, like the water flowing in wells beneath the surface of the earth. When you go through your day being at one with whatever you are doing, all of life becomes an art form. You feel the sensations of water on your body when you bathe, the taste and texture of the food you eat, the mental focus while driving, the heightened sensitivity when making love. The more your receptors are attuned to your experience, the more you are in contact with your true nature. A string of thoughts may amble through your mind, but you don't need to grab hold of them; you can let them pass like clouds.

> When we do something with a quiet, simple, clear mind, we have no notion or shadows, and our activity is strong and straightforward. But when we do something with a complicated mind, in relationship to other things, people, or society, our activity becomes very complex.
>
> —SHUNRYU SUZUKI, *ZEN MIND, BEGINNER'S MIND*

Beginner's mind is free of judgments, dogma, and rules, a mind unclouded by stereotypes, interpretations, and expectations.

Having a beginner's mind means there's no agenda for the outcome; you are just following something deep inside. With a beginner's mind you can show up for where life takes you rather than writing a script. Your interactions or activities will have a freshness to them. Even if you chop vegetables every day, you notice their color, texture, and smell and delight in the composition of putting them all together.

This contrasts with doing things motivated by the ego self—seeking praise, definition, reward, or admiration, which will dissolve like cotton candy because they never truly satisfy. When we're driven by ego, we are aware of pressing against time, trying to get somewhere, trying to impress someone. When you're in a beginner's mind, time may seem to contract and expand. There is motion amid a state of calm. You start working on a project and suddenly five hours have passed. At the same time, everything may slow down or stretch out. For example, if you are playing tennis, you don't feel frantic; there's ample time to get in position, stroke the ball, and return to a relaxed state. There can be speed and motion without agitation.

Beginner's mind doesn't exclude ideas or thoughts; they arise on their own in the interest of what we are doing, but they are not those conditioned thoughts from the past. When we make love with a beginner's mind we can explore, touch, feel, attune, whisper, and respond as if making love for the first time, yet with the ancient wisdom of love flowing through our veins.

Having a beginner's mind also allows us to develop parts of ourselves we never dreamed we had, like waking up a sleeping giant within. Recently I attended a stunning voice concert of a woman in her thirties. Six years previously, she had casually gone for a few voice lessons after having difficulty singing the high notes in her church choir. Her teacher, astounded by the lovely quality of her singing, referred her to a local professor who, after a few lessons, suggested she apply to study at the university. Three years later, degree in hand, she left to study abroad and is now building a career as a professional singer. You never know what gifts are roaming around inside you.

There's an expression, "God is in the details." As any artist or creative person knows, a beautiful product is the result of talent, practice, careful attention to details, and diligence. But likewise, creativity also flows from letting go of all these things and being in the experience, in an egoless energy field of delight and happiness.

EXERCISE:

Experience Beginner's Mind

1. Recall a time where you felt deeply engaged in an activity and time passed either very quickly or seemed to slow down. Notice how your body feels when you focus on this memory. Stay focused on the feelings and let the memory fade away.

2. Beginner's Mind Question. (Also known as the Quantum Question by Stephen Wolinsky.) For a momentary experience of Zen mind, beginner's mind, ask yourself the following question—read it very slowly, imagining you let go of memory and mind.

   "Without language, memory, mind, interpretations, or expectations what is . . . happiness?"

   What happens? If you truly have stepped beyond language, memory, and so on, you will feel a momentary blankness or void. Let yourself fall into it. Float in it. Then use the same question substituting other words such as guilt, shame, joy, love, anger, and goodness for happiness.

3. Over the course of a day observe as you move between a relaxed mind—beginner's mind—and when you're operating with your ego—tense and grasping. Notice thoughts and body sensations.

13. Take the Journey of a Thousand Steps: Do One Small Thing

What typifies people who don't lose heart or get depressed, even in spite of a challenging life, is that they can focus on simple, small things that can be done on a daily basis. Typically they *do not* dwell on the difficulty of their situation. As Helen told me, "I was single, parenting three children, separated from my husband, going to school, and living on a small income. But I never wanted the children to feel bad, so I thoughts of lots of little ways to make life fun, interesting, and keep us close."

It could be something as simple as buying one flower for the dining table, a child's bar of soap with a pleasing scent, snuggling up and reading to the children (and not stopping to answer the phone), hanging a pretty scarf over the corner of a picture, having a cup of hot chocolate, or going out to look at the stars. It could also involve learning or developing a passionate interest in something like drawing, reading, or teaching.

Buddhism is about living now, about the quality, peace, and beauty of every day, about breathing life into the moment. This does not require a lot of money. Just creating one little spark can energize your cells and create a shift inside. And if we do it often, it adds up to significant change.

The Butterfly Effect, often spoken of in Buddhist circles, suggests that every thought, every act, even as tiny as the wings of a butterfly, sets off a vibration that is felt around the world. Whatever you do matters.

Try some of these suggestions for showing up for life:

- Start singing around the house . . . or chant Om.
- Talk with someone at a checkout stand.
- Call, go visit, or send a card to someone who is lonely or ill and wish them the best.
- Pick out a bright or strong paint color and get a friend to help you paint an accent wall in your living space.
- Go shopping with a friend and try on clothes you thought you would never wear. Buy something in a color you've seldom worn.
- Go to the library or a bookstore and read from a few books on subjects that intrigue you.
- Call a friend from the past who has recently come to mind (they may be only a Google away) and say hello, you're thinking about them.
- Go to a thrift store and get something playful, totally fun, like red satin lacy pajamas, a stylish old dress, or a striped suit vest.
- Sign up for a class in something, from exercise to cake decorating to CPR, possibly at a community learning center.
- Call a friend and offer to do an exchange so you can get some help with a task that has you stuck—clearing out old clothes, cleaning up the garage, painting a room, talking about your fears.
- Start playing or learning a musical instrument.
- Swap child care so you have some free time.
- Volunteer at a community agency or school.

On the introspective side you could:

- Get up five minutes earlier and do some deep breathing and stretching.
- Sit down for five minutes, breathe with a relaxed belly, and scan your body—as if there was a little you with a flashlight inside—noticing whatever you are feeling physically and emotionally.
- Take ten minutes a day to focus on gratitude.

- Sit down and drink a cup of tea and look out the window, and focus on your breathing.
- Write about anything that comes to you for fifteen minutes a day.
- Buy a yoga, Pilates, or other exercise tape and follow it for at least fifteen minutes, three times a week.
- Meet a friend on a regular basis to go for a walk.

Do these things to spark your energy, wake yourself up, and expand the universe of your life.

Pay Attention

14. Be a Scientist About Your Life

> Listen friend, this body is his dulcimer.
> He draws the strings tight, and out of it comes
> the music of the inner universe.
> —KABIR, 44 ECSTATIC POEMS

Kabir's words, "this body is his dulcimer . . . out of it comes the music of the inner universe," underscores that being attuned to yourself means being as one with the music of the universe, the essence of who you are. In other words, we pay attention to ourselves to find out our own rhythms and harmonies. If you've ever watched a piano tuner, he taps a Y-shaped piece of metal that vibrates at 440 beats per second, which is the sound called A, then he holds it to his ear while he plays A on the piano. Then he puts a tuning wrench on the string pins and makes minute adjustments in the tension until the A string is a pure 440 vibrations per second.

When you show up to the world around you, you come in contact with many ideas, thoughts, and possibilities. When you take the next step and pay close attention, you attune to your body, mind, sensations, and emotions, which together give you a starting place for being wise in the world. In Buddhism, paying attention is often referred to as mindfulness and is the seventh step of the Eightfold Path. That sudden tension in your neck, sense of uneasiness, or feeling of calm are the convergence of thousands of signals moving from outside you to inside and back again. To be mindful is to notice them, pay attention, and use them as information.

For example, if you routinely feel drained or uneasy around a certain person, you have important data for making future decisions. Instead of analyzing the person, you make the connection: "If I'm around so and so, I feel drained and uneasy." You can attempt to find a way to change your experience, but if that fails, it's up to you to make an informed choice based on reality. If you have a judging, analyzing mind, it may create a lot of interference by trying to figure out why, making excuses, or suddenly feeling guilty—"I *should* be strong enough to handle it, I'm mean to go away." It takes courage to start trusting the instrument of you, but the more you bring together the many aspects of yourself, including your impulses, physical sensations, intuition, and wisest mind, the more informed your decisions will be.

Paying attention means becoming a scientist about your mental habits. When your inner voices are competing in a jumble of confusion, you can slow them down, take them apart, and listen to each one. Okay, let's see. 1) I'm really upset in this relationship. 2) But I'm afraid of making a mistake if I leave. 3) I'd feel like a failure, I've messed up so many relationships. 4) Geez, I'm wanting some candy. 5) If I can just shift my attitude maybe it will all work. 6) I'm sleepy. I have my clients go into each part and explore everything it has to say, and then start having a conversation with each other. So much of getting unstuck involves slowing down whatever is going on inside so you can bring it all on screen and explore it. You quiet down the mental jumble and confusion by taking it apart.

The piano tuner can't hear the vibration of the tuning fork if people are shouting, playing loud music, or interrupting with questions. Similarly, to attune to your real nature, you need to clear the clutter, noise, and tension of your mind and drop into stillness. From this place you see more clearly, feel more relaxed, and are better able to follow a path that is true to you.

Paying attention starts at a very basic level, by noticing when you are hungry, sleepy, uneasy, need to eliminate, want to be with people or alone. To flow with these needs is the starting point for integrating your body, mind, and emotions. You fine tune the instrument that is you so it can go from notes to melodies.

15. Pay Attention to the Eight Worldly Winds

As you're in the process of finding the music of who you are it is easy to be pulled off course. In Buddhism these common influences are known as the Eight Worldly Winds.

Pleasure and pain,
gain and loss,
praise and blame,
fame and shame.

Take a moment to ponder how these influences shape your life. Which of the winds tend to throw you off center the most? Don't forget to focus on both sides of the equation, such as praise *and* blame, because whatever takes you up can also take you down. The ego is being inflated either way. For example, what happens when you are blamed and criticized? Do you crumble and feel lousy about yourself for hours? This magnifies your self-absorption just as much as feeling elated over praise and adulation, because neither one means anything about the spirit of who you are. When you are blown off center by these worldly winds, you become the candle in the wind— you lose your grounding. You are measuring yourself on a scale of variable worth, which is sure to fluctuate and cause you to suffer.

Why are fame and shame paired together? To seek fame is usually an attempt to run from deep feelings of being bad, unlovable, or ashamed of who you are. The more you seek fame the more the shame churns inside because you are ensnared in the ego, which believes fame will make you happy. When seeking is driven by the ego, it is always accompanied by fear—fear of not having enough, of not succeeding, of losing what you've gained and having the dreaded shame come spilling out all over you. You then have the choice to run harder in a new direction or sit down, make friends with your shame, and get out of the race.

You might notice if the worldly winds are central to your whole life, or an occasional puff of wind. Notice the intensity and duration of your reactions when you are disappointed. Do you have a momentary upset that quickly dissipates, or are you still grumbling and constricted hours, or even days, after feeling the wind? This is a good indicator of how much your ego is hooked on the outcome of a situation.

To step beyond the grasp of the Eight Worldly Winds, you can start by paying attention to the suffering they create and how they affect all aspects of your being. For example, take fame/status/money: to gain fame you might overwork, put on a mask to impress people, create an image, or buy special clothes. Your internal dialogues will be intense and driven. You are strategizing, planning, worrying, hoping. Your breathing, which becomes shallow as a result, affects your ability to relax, which leads to internal tension. If you don't achieve the fame you want you feel angry and blame others. This alienates your relationship and you feel alone, and to soothe the emptiness you drink too much alcohol. There is so much suffering in this scenario because it lacks joy, passion, and heart. Be aware of all the links to suffering when you are in the throes of the Eight Worldly Winds.

Remember, every breath, thought, word, and action is part of a hologram called life, which is within you and everything around you. When you are enjoying a breeze but not getting blown off course by the worldly winds, you become more deeply embedded in your humanity and feel an enduring calm. When we treasure life and feel awe and wonder for the essence of creation, we can step away from these external pulls and come back home to ourselves.

The shelter from the Eight Worldly Winds is mindfulness, awareness, fascination, and curiosity. It's about paying attention to physical sensations, internal dialogues, energy levels, and emotional states. It's about being fully engaged with whatever you are doing, deeply attuned to other people, and taking part to ease injustice and suffering in the world. It's about finding out who you are rather than trying to "be" something. It's about giving up the praise, gain, fame, and pleasures that lead to grasping, tension, and losing track of your true self. It's to swim against the stream of what we've often been told, and to treasure your life and how it feels to relax, be touched by beauty, develop your talents, and feel your connections to others.

16. Find Your Observer, Your Timeless Friend

> *Discover all you are not. Body, feelings, thoughts, ideas, time, space, being and not-being . . . nothing concrete or abstract you can point out to is you. You must watch yourself continuously— particularly your mind—moment by moment, missing nothing. This witnessing is essential for the separation of the self from the not-self.*
>
> —SRI NISARGADATTA MAHARAJ, *I AM THAT*

Being able to relax into awareness requires the ability to observe or witness yourself. Ultimately we realize that the observer and the observed arise and fall together, but the initial step is to develop the ability to witness or observe oneself. For example, let's say a part of you reacts to a situation on automatic—same old upset and words— and another part notices what's occurring. Aha, there's that old reaction. I'm really getting upset and defensive—what is that *really* about? Bringing awareness to the situation creates spaciousness and the possibility for change. It's a far different experience to say, "Wow, I'm having a big case of neediness or jealousy," than to fall completely into the grip of neediness or jealousy as if they're your complete identity.

The observer is loosely engaged in whatever is happening but also has a laid back feeling as she notices your breathing, the ways your body gets tight, how you get insistent or afraid, or how you want to run away from feelings. The observer also notices red flags, wiggles of doubt, and uneasiness when you are considering a major change, perhaps a new job or relationship. It gives you the keys to being wary and wise. The observer helps you experience yourself as a dynamic, changing process, not a fixed identity. This awareness takes you beyond your concrete identification with the self to appreciating the temporal, ever-changing nature of the mind, emotions, and desires.

The kindly observer or witness realizes your dance is created by your conditioning and nervous system, so instead of taking it seriously the observer watches as if it were a drama or movie: there goes my conditioned self jumping to conclusions, changing moods, making interpretations. The observer can learn to notice when you're holding your breath, shutting down, not talking. Instead of being swamped in depression, you observe the depression as happening while realizing that your essence exists apart from the depression. Similarly, you may have an addiction, but you are not only an addiction. This doesn't mean you ignore the depression or addiction or don't seek remedies for it. It means that you don't personalize it in relation to your "worth," and you don't add layers of guilt and shame, as in I shouldn't be depressed or I shouldn't be addicted.

If you become distracted and preoccupied, you can observe that, "Wow, my mind is sure wandering around." It's like throwing out a line and reeling yourself back to center instead of spiraling off into speeding thoughts and agitation. Developing your observer means tapping into your consciousness, which is timeless and non-judgmental, a wise friend to guide you.

It's important to understand that observing oneself creates a dynamic process that forms a continuous circle. In other words, the observer affects the observed. This concept stems from physicist Werner Heisenberg's assertion that in the subatomic world to observe a phenomenon is to change it. Likewise, when you bring awareness to a part of yourself that has operated on automatic pilot, you are bringing consciousness to what was formerly unconscious. You are creating the possibility of choice instead of feeling driven. Once observed, you can no longer repeat an action quite so unconsciously. This raises inner conflict: the "I want to sit around all day" part now has to contend with the part that says, "But I really planned to take a walk and get some exercise." The conflict will eventually dissipate as you more fully settle into conscious behavior.

In working with addictions, for example, I often counsel people to stay awake, stay aware. I might say, "If you're going to have an eating binge, invite a friend to be with you." This suggestion usually brings a look of astonishment because part of bingeing is perpetuating the shame cycle, which requires secrecy. Similarly, I tell people, if you are going out to try to seduce someone, be aware of what your heart is truly seeking, the strategies you use to seduce her/him, the con, the charm, the physical high, the experience of sex, how you feel afterward, and if you got what you were longing for. This, of course, interferes with the unconscious compulsive act, and is not always welcome. I've had more than one client irritated or outright angry at me for bringing consciousness to their addictive behavior. It messes up the game.

As you become the observer, or bring conscious awareness to your behavior, you may experience an inner rebel—"I don't want to have to think about everything I'm doing!" This journey of waking up does not come without effort, but it also can be quite amusing . . . if you observe yourself!

17. Clear Out the Chaos and Make Room for Life

The Zen masters have nothing to defend,
for the simple reason that they possess nothing.
—ZEN SAYING

Go Sweep out the chambers of your heart
make it ready, make it ready
to be the dwelling of The Beloved.
SUFI PEACE DANCE—MUHUMMED SHABISTARI

Living with constant chaos around us is like listening to static on the radio—we can never get a clear channel, we never hear the music or the beating of our own hearts. To make room for the Beloved, the spirit, a clear idea about our future, or our heart's delight, we need stillness and relaxation. Junk food, junk mail, junk thoughts, and just plain junk often get in the way of feeling calm.

Focus your awareness on the physical and emotional effects of a chaotic life. Are you often frustrated or cursing because you misplace the keys, run out of milk, trip over shoes in the front hall, or run out of clean underwear? Do piles, stacks, and overstuffed drawers get on your nerves on a daily basis? Do you tighten up or stress out when you get a penalty for a late bill, or do you plough through a crowded closet looking for a favorite shirt? Do you have to try three pens before you find one that writes? Notice the irritation and agitation that arise from these little pieces of chaos. While each part may seem small, added together over time it's like collecting little pebbles in your shoes.

Think of your body revving up in frustration—muscles and tendons constrict, stress hormones are secreted, and the receptors throughout your body feel the alarm. Think of this multiplied hundreds of times over your days, weeks, and years. What in your lifestyle and living space creates frustration? What creates calm? There is no one standard for clearing out chaos; it's about what creates chaos inside you.

Notice, by contrast, what transmits a sense of beauty and calm, either in your home or other people's homes. How do you feel? What colors, types of furnishings, lighting, plants, and spacing of furniture feels right for you?

Keeping your life cluttered is often a smoke screen obscuring a fear of emptiness or loneliness and a sense of unworthiness. The tendency to acquire too much stuff can come from various sources. Sometimes its about compulsive shopping, even if it's at the Goodwill. It can be about having a difficult time letting go of things. It can be about keeping our lives so messy we have no time, space, or energy to focus on the changes we need to make. Other times we collect stuff with the hope of feeling important, lovable, worthwhile, or secure.

Whatever the situation, ask yourself: "Is this the way I want my life? Does this stuff really make me happy, relaxed, content? Can I relax and feel rejuvenated here?" Having traveled in many countries, I have observed that people in the United States accumulate more stuff than people in most countries. His Holiness the Dalai Lama also observed that people in the United States, the land of power and "stuff," are the unhappiest people in the world. The primary antidote to our attachment to stuff is finding true connections with others, feeling a sense of belonging, and being of service.

When we have less to take care of, worry about, or lock up, life is simpler. I'm reminded of the lyrics, "I've got plenty of nothing and nothing's plenty for me," that Porgy sings after falling in love with Bess in the opera *Porgy and Bess*. Imagine not worrying if someone steals the rug from your floor because you feel so much joy in your love, and in the beauty of the world. Imagine the freedom of having just enough, of not worrying if something gets broken or lost.

Now here's the paradox. The idea of clearing out clutter is not to be confused with thoughts such as, "If I get rid of clutter, I'll be more spiritual." Some people with a sloppy house are warm and friendly, while some people are tense and controlling in a tidy house. It's about being aware of what stimulates frustration and takes you away from the aliveness that you are. It's about having a relaxing home base that gives respite so you can venture out in the world and contribute your very best. It's about making time for whatever brings joy, beauty, and depth to your life—in other words, whatever helps you become unstuck.

EXERCISE:

Reducing Chaos, Making Life Easier

1. Meet your security needs. Make sure you have food, shelter, clothing, heat, water, and gas for the car so you can get to work. It's difficult to relax when life is a constant succession of mostly preventable emergencies. So plan ahead and take care of the basics. I call this the "don't be surprised" level.

- Don't be surprised if your check bounces when you didn't make a deposit or you run out of grocery money because you spent it on three new videos.

- Don't be surprised when you get tense, sick, and irritable after working overtime for weeks at at time.

- Don't be surprised when friends drift away because you don't return phone calls or initiate getting together.

- Don't be surprised when your child acts out when you haven't played with him, taken him anywhere, held him, or shown pleasure in his company all weekend.

We're getting unstuck when we say, "Well, I guess I had it coming. I didn't take care of that, what do I expect!" We make a dramatic shift when we take responsibility for ourselves and get our lives, clutter, and chaos in order.

2. Schedule time to clear out excess possessions. It's good to have a friend to help.

3. Create a place for items you use daily—keys, shoes, wallet, toys, appointment book, gloves, bills, purse, maps, dirty clothes, and notice how it feels to lower the daily agitations. If you constantly misplace keys, get three extra sets made and make a place for them so you'll be able to find at least one. If one organizational plan doesn't work, try another. If it's difficult to get started, talk with other people about how they do it or go to a home show or building store.

18. Explore Your Amazing Mind

The mind of the sage does not abide anywhere . . .
not in goodness, evil, being, non-being, inside,
outside, or in the middle . . .

ROBERT LINSSEN, *LIVING ZEN*

Both noticing your mind and realizing you are not your mind lies at the heart of Buddhism. The Buddha considered the mind to be in the same category as the other senses: our task is to see its nature, how it is conditioned, and how it affects every level of our being. It is not that we fight our minds; rather, we wake up and see the rise and fall of thoughts and the role they play in our suffering as well as our joy and power.

Beneath your conditioned mind you have a powerful ability to direct energy and become a channel for knowledge, wisdom, and healing. On the other hand, the conditioned mind can race in circles with repetitive images and thoughts that can be irrational and fearful and lead us to agitation, emotional overload, and anxiety.

Here are two aspects of mind to consider: first is the conditioned mind made up of all we have been taught either overtly or covertly from family, culture, and social systems. It's the shoulds, rules, and judgments that sometimes seem like a train without breaks running through our heads. Whether we label them as positive—they help us reason and cope—or see them as the censors and critics that taunt us, the point is to remember they are all aspects of conditioning and are not who we really are. In other words, everything in your mind was put there one way or another.

The second aspect of the mind is the creative mind, which arises when we get out of the way and allow thoughts to emanate from stillness, fascination, curiosity, and interest. The creative mind is absorbed in the moment, engaged in something beyond the self. It's not completely separated from our conditioning, but it is not running on automatic. It's like the music playing through us, getting lost in time as we're tinkering with something to find a solution, the proverbial light bulb going off inside with the answer to a question we've been pondering. It's as if thoughts come to us from the Big Mind of the Universe, they just happen, rather than stemming from a desire to prove we are good, lovable, and worthwhile.

As you explore your conditioned mind in the next four chapters, you can ponder how it got you off course. This will help you understand how you can retrace your steps to come home to your natural self.

A road map for the journey: Here is a diagram that shows the path of getting stuck. I'll discuss it in the next three chapters.

False Core Beliefs and the Path of Getting Stuck

STRIVING
DISSATISFIED
FEAR
ALIENATION/EMPTINESS

ANXIETY
FEAR
LOSS OF SELF
WORRY

OPERATIONAL BELIEFS

I feel powerful when . . .
  I seduce someone
  I have control
  I have money

OPERATIONAL BELIEFS

I feel secure when . . .
  Someone takes care
    of me
  I am adored

BELIEFS TO REDUCE ANXIETY

  I don't need anyone
  I don't care about these people
  I can do it alone

BELIEFS TO REDUCE ANXIETY

Someday my prince (princess)
will come . . . If I'm good enough

DEPENDENCE/NEEDINESS
IS NOT OKAY

ANGER/POWER
IS NOT OKAY

FILTER

FACTORS IN DEVELOPING BELIEFS
culture, family, temperament, genetics, chance

CORE BELIEFS

I am defective
I am shameful
I am unlovable
I am worthless/inadequate
I am powerless/helpless
I will always be abandoned
I am invisible

SEPARATION/LOSS CONDITIONING

I Am

quantum field   life   void   emptiness   God   All That Is

19. Realize Your Connection to the Underlying Unity of All Life

Whatever we see is changing, losing its balance . . . but its background is always in perfect harmony. This is how everything exists in the realm of Buddha nature—losing its balance against a background of perfect balance.

—SHUNRYU SUZUKI, ZEN MIND, BEGINNER'S MIND

On the journey of getting unstuck and breaking free, being aware of the unifying energy from which all life is created can become a peaceful background to the drama of our lives. When we get caught up in the minutia of the everyday, we can drop into this vast space and remember that our little dramas are played out against the expanse of all time. Said another way, this moment matters at one level, but at another it's not cosmically serious.

From the mystics, to Buddhism, to Einstein, to Sufism, to Christianity, to quantum physics, we have the assertion that all of life comes from one energy, One Substance, or Emptiness. It can be called chi, prana, quantum field, God, Yaweh, All That Is, or the Unifying Field. All creation is emptiness or energy condensing down into form. It's a constant process of transformation. In Albert Einstein's words, "Matter can neither be created nor destroyed, it can only be transformed." The seed of the tree draws on the one energy manifest as air, water, soil, and sunshine and condenses to form the trunk, branches, and leaves. A thought can condense at various levels, from a passing idea, to a nagging irritation, to intense berating of ourselves.

To better understand this concept, imagine the ocean representing All That Is or the One Substance of the Universe. Then, imagine your lifespan as a tiny bubble that forms on the surface—still part of the ocean but with a separate identity. You go through your life as a bubble, bobbing around on the ocean, having your particular ride on the waves or time spent sitting in a bog. When you "die"—or, you might say, when your bubble pops—you dissolve back into the ocean. At one level you were a separate bubble with a separate lifespan, and at another level you were always part of the One Energy.

What does this have to do with getting unstuck in life? It reminds you that you're part of something bigger, a force beyond your comprehension. You can bring attention to the dance of today while simultaneously remembering that you're passing through a moment in the cosmic scope of time. You are, always have been, and always will be, part of the One Substance of the Universe. This perspective gives you a touchstone to help you remember the temporal nature of your physical body, emotions, joys, and thoughts. It brings deeper meaning to the phrase, "This, too, shall pass." We're part of the One Substance that can neither be created nor destroyed.

EXERCISE:

Ponder the One Substance That Is Eternal

With the following exercises, notice any internal shifts you feel—lighter, heavier, confused, relaxed, and so on. Also notice any ego resistance.

1. Pay attention to what happens when you narrow your vision and get completely upset by a problem—it becomes intense, dramatic, do or die. Then notice what happens if you drop back and ponder that you are part of the field of All That Is, the One Substance, and this too shall pass. Now see if you can hold on to both realities at the same time.

2. Ponder the enigmatic question posed by Nisargadatta Maharaj, "Eight days prior to conception, were you?"

3. Look up at the stars, or imagine them. Think of the stars, the space between all the universes, all the people on this earth, the trees, water, everything, as made of one substance condensed down into different forms. Then, as you are sitting in a room, or outside in the daylight, think of the empty space between everything as energy and made from the same substance as the objects you see.

4. Look at a table, chair, book, rug, or whatever, and contemplate its history, going back to the time it was emptiness. For example, start with a piece of wooden furniture, go back to when it was a board, then a tree, then not yet a tree, just a seedling, then the sun, rain, earth, and air that helped energy condense into the growing tree.

20. Feel the Ease: You Are Born into the "I Am"

> When you become you, Zen becomes Zen.
> When you are you, you see things as they are,
> and you become one with your surroundings.
> —SHUNRYU SUZUKI, ZEN MIND, BEGINNER'S MIND

You are born. You are a Zen baby because you live totally in the present—the world of "I Am," a concept taught by Nisargadatta. You exist without language, interpretations, or labels. You are a little sensorimotor creature motivated by hunger, discomfort, and need for human connection in the form of affection, holding, feeding, cooing, and eye contact. In fact, for the first five or six months you are like a kangaroo baby because you experience yourself as merged with your mother.

In this state of be-ing, if you are hungry or need soothing, you cry. If you are sleepy you sleep. As you start to crawl, you go in the direction of whatever intrigues you—a stuffed animal, a red block, a puppy dog. Your creativity has no rules—you rip up tissue paper, explore what's in the trash, put things in your mouth, take things apart, and cuddle up to a blanket in your caretaker's arms. You don't have language or concepts about right-wrong, pretty-ugly, good-bad. Nisargadatta, in *I Am That*, speaks of this wordless "I Am" and its relationship to consciousness. "Naming cannot go beyond the mind, while perceiving is consciousness itself . . . you are and I am. But only as points in consciousness; we are nothing apart from consciousness. This must be well grasped; the world hangs on the thread of consciousness; no consciousness, no world."

Thus in the "I Am" we are one with consciousness and feel no separation from the One Substance of the Universe. There is no sense of a separate self.

The "I Am" is that place of simply being. It is spontaneous, creative, receptive, and open, unhindered by rigid shoulds, rules, concepts, and fixed beliefs. It is where we all began life. It is the place of our humanity—where pure love exists. From the "I Am," we see into the heart of all things. We experience awe and wonder. It is the place most people long to return to when they embark on a spiritual journey.

EXERCISES:

Experience the Wordless "I Am"

1. *Remember a time you were completely lost or engrossed in something you were doing,* when time slid by, your mind was quiet and deeply focused on whatever you were doing. Take a deep breath. Take time to drift back there. How does your body feel? Notice the focus of your mind.

2. *Pick up a beautiful crystal, pen, or object and simply experience it without any descriptive words.* Hold it, turn it over, touch it in different ways, tap it, smell it, play with it. If your minds starts to analyze or describe it, quietly take a breath and come back to simply experiencing it. With time you will find yourself staying longer in a wordless fascinated state. As you stay with the experience you will find there is more and more to explore.

3. *Throughout the day, focus on the phrase "I Am," and drop everything that follows.* Thus, if thoughts of I Am . . . clumsy, stupid, smart, or talented arise in your mind, gently disconnect them, take a breath, and say to yourself *"I Am."*

> *And if the earthly has forgotten you,*
> *say to the still earth: I flow.*
> *To the rapid water speak: I am.*
> —RAINER MARIA RILKE, SONNETS TO ORPHEUS, II, 29

21. Step Out of the Garden: Notice the Power of False Core Beliefs

Between the ages of five to nine months, to our dismay we find we are not merged with our mother nor are we the center of her universe. We are separate! She has other people in her life. Terror strikes at our young heart. People start saying, "No, don't do that," and sometimes we are frustrated, unhappy, or scared, and no one comes. We are cast out of the paradise of "I Am."

The level of our distress is deeply affected by the ability of our caregivers to attune to our sounds, gestures, and needs. Our distress is eased greatly when we are cradled in loving arms, mirrored, and looked at with delight by our primary caregiver who feels relaxed in his or her body.

If we are routinely neglected, hurt, hit, or shamed, or we observe violence, our nervous systems will be chronically agitated and our false core beliefs will become deeply rooted in our psychological make-up. At worst they become like a Goliath looming over us, storming about inside, criticizing, censoring, mercilessly harping at us, convincing us we are unlovable or a loser. The tenacity and pervasiveness of our false core beliefs will vary tremendously.

Even in the best of situations, however, we need to deal with the prospect of being a separate human being, along with the reality that we are completely helpless and unable to care for ourselves. It might go something like this—unconsciously, of course. "Oh my gosh, I'm no longer merged with my mother, this is scary. I must have done something wrong, how can I get her back? I'd better do whatever it takes to make sure she stays with me." (Does this sound a bit like what happens in lover relationships?) The child wanting to feel merged instead of separate comes to a conclusion about what went wrong or what he or she can do to once again feel merged.

Here are some core beliefs that start to emerge:*

I am defective	My body is defective or shameful
I am shameful	I am worthless
I am unlovable	I am inadequate
I am powerless over my life	I don't exist
I am unwanted	I am alone
I will always be abandoned	

See which beliefs ring true for you. While most of us have some aspects of these false core beliefs, there is usually one in particular that

---

*The last four beliefs come from workshops with Stephen Wolinsky.

becomes the central belief around which we organize our personality. This concept of a single organizing personality trait derives from historic Sufi teachings, which became the Enneagram.

Culture, Family, and Genetic Filter

The formation of our false core beliefs is a process affected by millions of interactions over the years with our parents, families, and social system. It's a combination of what happens around us and what we bring to a situation—our perceptions and internal reactions and conclusions we come to—that become our belief system and ways of coping. We bring to the table an exquisite mix of genetics, temperament, education, intelligence, physical ability, chance events, and cultural messages affected by class, race, and ethnic background.

As survival creatures, we tend to adopt types of behavior and skills that help us fit in, gain approval, get attention, and avoid harm or rejection. In some families acceptance is readily given, in others we find ourselves fighting against parental scripts, and in yet others we seek ways to survive chaos, insensitivity, and violence.

As we slip away from the state of "I Am," we enter the world of language—of good and bad, right and wrong, acceptable and not acceptable. Language, beliefs, and fitting in begin to overshadow the simplicity and peacefulness of "I Am."

Two Diverging Paths

We tend to veer off from the natural self in two different ways. Some people deny their power, anger, strength, and right to self-expression and seek security through others—I'll be rescued, some day my prince/princess will come. Other people deny their need for human connection, affiliation, care, and support and take on the stance, you can't count on anyone, I can do it myself. Many people do some of both. In either case, the person becomes fragmented because they are denying various parts of themselves, from their intelligence, ability to act, and need for affiliation, to their anger, fear, and grief. Instead of being in the flow of life, they spend their energy pushing away and hiding various parts of themselves. This leads to self-absorption and feeling separate, which creates anxiety.

Stories to Reduce Anxiety or Uneasiness

The people who deny their power, strengths, and self-expression tend to feel insecure and look for someone to take care of them. It sounds a bit like the fairy tales—I'll feel secure when I find someone who adores me, when I'm told I'm beautiful and I have a nice home to live in. The stories often center around some magical, unlikely event taking place that will ease all of one's suffering and make life sweet and easy. From finding the all-loving or rich partner, to winning the lottery, to a dreamy notion that things will just get better on their own. It's like living with one foot off the ground, not realizing the need to be proactive in one's own life.

The "I don't need anyone" (or "I won't let anyone get close to me") side might feel like, "I am strong, I can cope, I can figure it out myself, and I don't need anyone." As a result a person might become extremely skilled in a profession yet be uneasy and afraid in relationships— emotionally and physically walled off from the ability to love and be loved. "I must do it myself," is a natural conclusion to come to if early relationships have been fraught with hurt, loneliness, and inconsistency. But the truth is, we all need relationships and a sense of belonging to feel at ease in life.

Either type of story makes us feel uneasy and off center and we wind up losing access to crucial aspects of ourselves. Creating a pattern of behavior to try to cope with or compensate for the anxiety-producing beliefs is the result.

Compensating Beliefs or Behaviors

To avoid pain and anxiety, we transform our false core beliefs into a course of action. Usually through a period of trial and error we create a system of beliefs and behaviors that provide an illusory escape from the dreaded feelings associated with our false core beliefs. The problem is that they don't work because concepts such as lovable, worthwhile, powerful, and shameful are mental constructs based on conditioning and are not who we really are. In other words, you can't disprove something that doesn't exist to begin with.

Stephen Wolinsky teaches that all these concepts come in pairs. For example, the concept "I'm worthwhile" is inextricably tied to the concept of "I'm worthless." Why would you need to prove you are worthwhile if you didn't have a sense of being worthless? Both are abstract, subject to interpretation, and based on external circumstances, which means they can fluctuate moment to moment. Our journey to getting unstuck means dropping all these concepts and, as Nisargadatta teaches, meditate on the "I Am," and drop everything that follows. Give up trying to feel lovable, wanted, powerful, good, or worthwhile, and come back to the breath and the knowledge that you simply are. But I digress. Here's how we take a false core belief and try to overcome, hide, bury, or get rid of it to our peril.

Lost in the Spin of Disproving False Core Beliefs

FALSE CORE BELIEF	COMPENSATING BELIEF/BEHAVIOR
I am powerless	I feel powerful when I am the head of the organization
	I feel powerful when I seduce someone
	I feel powerful when I earn a lot of money
	I feel powerful when I look good
	I feel powerful when I have expensive things
I am unlovable	I feel lovable when someone admires me
	I feel lovable when I have sex
	I feel lovable when someone praises me
	I feel lovable when I get invitations from important people

FALSE CORE BELIEF   COMPENSATING BELIEF/BEHAVIOR

I am worthless

I feel worthwhile when I achieve

I feel worthwhile when people notice me

I feel worthwhile when I get an award

I feel worthwhile when I earn a lot of money

I feel worthwhile when I accomplish tasks

I feel worthwhile when I help others

I feel worthwhile when I'm good

I am helpless

I feel secure when someone takes care of me

I feel secure when I seduce someone

I feel secure when my children do well

I feel secure when I have a lot of money

I feel secure when people praise me

I feel secure when I believe God loves me

All these compensating behaviors create suffering because you're trying to prove or disprove a false belief about yourself. For example, if you're doing good deeds to prove you are worthwhile, there will be a driven quality about it. Being truly helpful flows naturally from an open heart. It's the difference between feeling relaxed and fascinated with life, as opposed to being driven by and operating out of the ego.

The ego is nearly always trying to expand itself. You praise me, my children do well, I earn a lot of money, and I feel bigger. But, like taking a drink or eating fudge, the momentary satisfaction is fleeting because the praise, the stellar behavior of your children, or the status of your job has nothing to do with the essence of who you are. The Buddha and the sages are never trying to build themselves up and, as a result, they are not tossed around by external events, situations, and the reactions of others. They lived centered in the constant and unified field of All That Is.

Caught in the Trap! Proving False Core Beliefs True and Untrue

While some people tend to drive themselves to disprove their false core beliefs, others tend to repeatedly prove they are true. Still others go back and forth between the two. For example, Alan spoke of trying to prove he was worthwhile by training for a better job. He passed twenty-one out of twenty-two tests to be certified in medical billing but never turned in the final test. He felt distracted, then paralyzed, and made up all kinds of reasons. On the surface it seems almost unbelievable, but if you understand the push-pull between I'm worthwhile and I'm worthless it all makes sense. He started out to prove he was worthwhile, but the I'm worthless side eventually sabotaged him. Even the offer of a friend to treat him to dinner and a night out if he finished was not sufficient to override the power of the worthless beliefs lodged deep within him. That's the strength of our unconscious beliefs, the reason we start the diet and stop, why fitness centers are crowded the first few weeks in the new year and by Valentine's day it's back to the regulars.

Whenever we're operating out of a false core belief, we risk sabotaging ourselves by getting on an endless treadmill, spinning between opposing parts vying for control. Our journey out of the trap is to realize these beliefs are false. They feel real, and they are deeply lodged inside, but if we can learn to step beyond them, like walking out of a force field, we can make changes.

If our friend Alan had realized a false core belief—a saboteur—was creeping into the picture, he could have named it instead of colluding with it by making up reasons and excuses. He could have realized that finishing the course didn't prove anything about his worth. It was just a way to make his life easier. He also could have mustered support internally and said, "I'm going to get past this saboteur and do something good for myself."

Caught in the Spin of False Core Beliefs

We have lost our way. The ego, which thinks the false core beliefs are true and real, has taken up residence in our mind. We've drifted away from the peaceful state of "I Am," with its spontaneity and ease, and ended up in a spinning trap, tangled up in the dance of proving and disproving we're good, lovable, worthwhile, powerful, or useful. To do this we've donned masks, created an image of ourselves, worked until we dropped, or have felt constant paralysis when we try to take charge of our lives. As a result we might feel anxious, depressed, and unhappy.

No matter how much money you accumulate, how big your successes, how many people you seduce, how many good deeds you do, no action or force of will can ever dispel the uneasiness stemming from a false core belief, for the simple reason that it's false to begin with, just a concept or illusion. You can't disprove something that is false to begin with. You can't run away from it, overcome it, or conquer it—you have to meet it face to face and realize it's all fiction. Gradually, while the thoughts may arise, you won't grab hold of them, take them so seriously, or let them stab you in the heart.

22. Separate Your True Self from Your Created Image—A Road Map

To become unstuck, you need to develop a deep awareness of how you are driven by your false core beliefs. Start by noticing which ones ring most true for you. There might be more than one. In workshops we imagine going through a day in the life of a false core belief. For example, you could take the belief, "I'm inadequate," or "I need to prove I am adequate" and track your day. What are your first thoughts when you wake up, what do you think about in the shower, what do you say to yourself if you have a bad hair day or nip yourself while shaving or trip over the dog dish? How does your false core belief relate to what you choose to wear or eat, or how much time you take in the morning?

Go through the day also noticing how this belief drives your thoughts—how much you caretake others, berate yourself, rationalize, blame others, try to convince yourself you're okay, feel guilty, and so on. The purpose of becoming aware is to step back from your actions and thoughts so it's more like watching the making of a movie. You don't just see the drama; you see the director, the camera, and all the props. It shifts the whole effect.

The false core belief comes out of hiding. Sometimes we coast along, keeping our false core belief submerged, only to be swamped by it in a time of stress or crisis. This reality hit Shannon full force when, after fulfilling her dream of owning a home and having enough money and a secure job, everything fell apart. Shannon had taken a job at the IRS as a poor single mother, hoping the money and health benefits would bring her a secure life and dispel her feelings of worthlessness. The job provided financial security and helped keep the worthless feelings at bay so long as everything was going right—pay raises, excellent job reviews, having money to pay the bills. Even so, there was always an undercurrent of anxiety and fear of the possibility of losing her position and being once again engulfed in the pain she had tried to escape.

Twenty-seven years later, hating the job, feeling desperate and torn between quitting and losing a lot of her retirement benefits or suffering through three more years, Shannon started getting depressed and having backaches and restless sleep. Going to work had become like entering enemy lines, as she was being shunned for not being "a good team player." She had become less rigid about her work, meaning that she had become more forgiving of poor people and those whose lives would be wrecked by severe penalties when she was in a position to make judgments on claims for past taxes.

As a result, the administration had flown two men in from Washington to "confront her." In her words, "They were there to tell me without a shred of kindness all the things I was doing wrong. It was pure intimidation." She went on to say, "I felt demolished, and horrible, like I was a terrible person. I couldn't get it off my mind." The tears welled up in her eyes as she brought both hands to her chest and leaned forward. "For days I've kept working to believe I'm a good, lovable, worthwhile person. All weekend at the Sufi retreat with lots of wonderful people trying to be helpful and saying good things about me, but the horrible feelings and thoughts just wouldn't go away." Her pain was palpable.

Shannon was caught in a familiar trap. She was trying to counteract thoughts of being bad and worthless with thoughts of being worthwhile and good. Here is why she couldn't convince herself: the thought of being worthless was her false core belief. To attempt to disprove what was false gave the belief the status of existence. In other words, if you believe you can be worthwhile, you also have to believe you can be worthless. Unwittingly, her friends had bought into the game and tried to convince her she was good, which only made her feel worse. She needed to see that it was all a drama superimposed on her true essence.

Shannon's next step was to extricate herself from the trap of believing that her deeply entrenched concepts of being lovable and worthwhile were real. That doesn't mean it wasn't painful and difficult to have the IRS loyalists undermining twenty-seven years of exemplary work, but the enduring pain came from holding to her negative beliefs about herself. Her solution was to get some inkling that worthwhile and worthless were only concepts, realize she was being unfairly treated, get support from friends, and stand up to the situation, which she eventually did. She was far less distraught after that and within a few months left the job.

Look at Your Own Road Map

When you can separate your constructed self full of concepts and beliefs from your true self, life will feel more relaxed and manageable. It will also feel a lot less serious because you will be able to joke about yourself.

There are four basic questions to ask yourself:

1. What beliefs about myself am I trying to prove or disprove?

2. What behaviors are a result of these beliefs?

3. Are these behaviors helping to create peace of mind, ease, and happiness?

4. What would happen if I gave up trying to prove anything?

The next step is to look at costs of being controlled by your false core beliefs. For example:

- Are you seeking for the key to becoming enlightened?
- To prove you are worthwhile, have you done things that have compromised your health and well-being?
- Have you spent countless hours and lots of money on your self-image—as hip, classy, beautiful, or powerful?
- To prove you are lovable or to not feel alone, have you stayed in painful relationships?
- Have you given up attempting to have intimate relationships to avoid facing loss?

- To prove you are powerful, do you seeks positions of power and become demanding and impatient with others?

- Do you feel sabotaged whenever you start to do something good for yourself? (You may get tired, want to run away, feel discouraged, or think it's impossible.)

- Do you feel guilty or worried about losing someone's love when you start to be honest or do something positive for yourself?

- Do you feel guilty or anxious for taking a day off for pleasure?

- Whatever you're seeking, do you keep needing more of it, be it validation, money, sex, accolades, possessions, drugs, or excitement?

- Are you a perfectionist? Do you feel terrible if you make mistakes or someone disapproves of you? Do you blame others if something goes wrong?

- Do you need to have power over others, to be in control to prevent feeling uneasy or vulnerable? Are you upset if someone challenges your authority?

- Do you feel either one up or one down? Do you judge or feel judged? Do you rarely feel on par with other people and able to relax into a spontaneous connection? Do you feel ambivalent in many situations?

- Does your sense of feeling okay rest on someone telling you repeatedly that they love you, care about you? But when they say it the uneasiness doesn't go away, and you need to hear it again, soon!

- Do you make lists to prove that you are good or worthwhile? I've helped others, been kind to dogs, given money to charity, and volunteered at the nursing home. (Unfortunately, many therapists and teachers suggest this.)

- Do you have a litany of negative thoughts streaming through your mind? I've messed up, I'm not good enough. No one will ever love me. I'll never get out of this lousy low-paying job and have a good life.

- Do you worry incessantly? What might go wrong? When will I have sex again? Is something wrong with my health? Where will I be in five years? Will my children be all right?

Throughout this process of examining your false core beliefs, I urge you to be profoundly merciful on yourself. These thoughts are hardwired into the nervous system and they persist until we observe, challenge, and loosen their grip.

> *Pure freedom is the essential law of the spirit. Freedom cannot "be conceived." It is lived, but it cannot be lived till concepts cease.*
> *The cessation itself is Liberty.*
> —ROBERT LINSSEN, *LIVING ZEN*

23. Feel the Freedom of Beginner's Mind

> *The beginner can know everything.*
> *The expert has no room to learn.*
> —ZEN SAYINGS

> *To live in the realm of Buddha nature means to die as a small being, moment after moment.*
> —SHUNRYU SUZUKI, *ZEN MIND, BEGINNER'S MIND*

Scenario: I'm in the hospital a few hours after surgery feeling virtually no pain as a result of several Reiki healing treatments. The doctor walks in and asks if I've had any painkillers. I tell her no, I'm feeling quite all right because some friends did a Reiki healing on me. Her eyes get that familiar glazed-over look that signals that her mind doesn't have any place to put my response. After a long pause she blurts out, "Well, you'll have more pain tomorrow!"

In a well known Zen story, an enthusiastic and smart university professor comes to an old Zen master for teachings. When the professor accepts the invitation to have tea, the Zen master pours the tea into his cup until it overflows. The Zen master keeps on pouring in spite of the obvious dismay of the professor. "A mind that is already full cannot take in anything new," the master explains. "Like this cup, you are full of opinions and preconceptions." To find happiness, you must first empty your cup.

When we are wedded to a belief system, we have no room to absorb ideas that are outside our experience. Everything is both referenced through our belief system and limited by it. The surgeon, a lovely, caring woman, had a single paradigm in her head about pain—you ease it with medication. Thus, the concept that I could have no pain as a result of a Reiki healing had no place to reside in her brain. If her mind had been empty, she could have been curious about the healing, and she wouldn't have needed to regain her equilibrium with a counterstatement that fit her belief system—surely I'd have pain by tomorrow.

Consider applying Shunryu Suzuki's words about dying as a small being, moment after moment, to your mind. Realize that whatever concepts you have in your mind are only that. Let them remain fluid and be ready to allow any of them to dissolve and float away if they create separateness with other people or are met with new information that expands your world. Most of all, don't equate your ideas with your identity or ego, for this is the source of arguments, and potentially even violence. My religion is better than your religion so I must defend it, even to death.

I am not saying it's inherently a problem to have ideas or opinions, even strongly held ones. It's when the ego attaches to one's ideas as one's identity that rigidity, closed-mindedness, and righteousness are likely to result. If you are identified with your beliefs, anything new that comes along is likely to bump into a "Do Not Disturb" sign on your head. That's because ideas that contradict our self-image throw off our equilibrium and disturb the sense of who we are. As a result we feel personally attacked, afraid, defensive, critical, rigid, and angry when people disagree with our beliefs.

When faced with new ideas you have two choices: either push them away so you don't disturb your mind, or dissolve your current beliefs to make room for something new. The latter is not easy because the ego identifies its very existence with its beliefs, and to let them go feels like something is dying. But it's a good death because it is your separate, small self that is dying.

It's often said that the sages have nothing to defend because their minds dwell in emptiness, beyond time and location. Imagine what it would be like to have an open, receptive mind or, for starters, not be attached to your beliefs. Have them, but don't defend them or identify with them. It is helpful to remember that all our beliefs are learned; we didn't have them when we were born.

Think of beginner's mind as the air you breathe. You feel open, light, and receptive. The muses feel free to fly in and out. You can't make them come, and you can't stop them from coming. You live connected to the great mind, or what is sometimes called Big Mind, which has a rhythm and pulse of its own.

If letting go of concepts and ideas is so creative and relaxing, why is it so hard? Think of a little boat lifting its anchor and floating down the river with no clear course. Think of believing that your life depends on that anchor holding you in place and you are terrified of losing control. That's the struggle we have until we experience letting go. To raise the anchor or let go of cherished beliefs and merge with the river is exactly how we die as a small being. We become free to notice the changing scenery along the river and be dazzled and delighted with the wonder of life.

When we drop out of the mind and stop holding, protecting, and defending our beliefs, we drop into our hearts and bodies. The best case for having a beginner's mind is that it's the only way to fully love and be loved. We don't love through ideas. We love through our beingness, resonance, breath, sensation, and ability to feel caring, understanding, and compassion, all with a light heart. Concepts divide us, but love, like the air we breathe, is beyond words, beyond the mind.

We all have certain deeply held beliefs that are hard to challenge. Read the following story and notice what happens in your mind. As an aside, after I had realized I included two examples of healing in this chapter, I thought, that's not "right"; I *should* only have one. Then another thought emerged: it's no problem—a beginner's mind allows whatever seems to flow. So just read the story and see what happens inside you.

Several years ago, my friend Carol and I attended a healing workshop on the power of thought, presented by Harold McCoy, director of the Ozark Research Institute. (I'll tell you more about him in the final section.) Carol, who has suffered from fibromyalgia for over ten years, volunteered to have Harold demonstrate his healing abilities on her in front of the class. At one point during the healing she said she felt something like a pleasant electrical current going all the way down her arms to her hands and through her body to her feet. It was as if something got re-wired inside. At the end of the healing she burst into tears of relief and was held by a close friend.

Within three months, the knots up and down her legs, neck, and shoulders literally unravelled, and she was no longer sensitive to touch. Her joint and muscle aches disappeared and her energy expanded tremendously to the point where she was able to do a ten-mile hike in Glacier Park. Three years later she is still completely well.

Notice what happened in your mind as you read this. Is there disbelief, skepticism, a desire to dismiss it as a chance happening, or is there interest, curiosity, and do you want Harold's phone number? It is fascinating to watch the reactions when Carol tells this story to the many people who ask about her fibromyalgia (she was bedridden and unable to move without intense pain at one point). People's eyes glaze over, or there's an "um-hmm" that precedes changing the subject. Rarely has anyone ever asked her to say more about her experience, and no one has ever asked how to contact Harold McCoy. Yet on the surface you'd think others would be eager to have such information. That's how powerful our mindset is in preventing new information from penetrating our being.

I summarize the case for a beginner's mind:

1. It's fun, playful, creative, and dynamic. You can play with ideas and creative solutions without getting defensive about them.

2. Fascination and curiosity displace guilt, shame, rigidity, platitudes, and a narrow perspective.

3. It's far more interesting than a preconditioned mind because it has room for subtleties, nuance, and fresh ideas. Your whole being becomes your language.

4. You become receptive and interested in other people rather than defensive, rigid, and afraid.

5. Your mind quiets down and you experience greater ease and calm.

6. A beginner's mind frees the heart and body to truly love.

> Soak all your prejudices in oil—
> I would consider it a favor.
> Bring and sing to me your darkest thoughts,
> For my whole body is a blazing emerald wick
> I am a pure flame
> Who needs and loves to burn your trash.
>
> —Hafiz, *The Gift*

Live in Reality, Listen to Your Truths

I believe that unarmed truth and unconditional love will have the final word in reality.
—MARTIN LUTHER KING, JR., WHY WE CAN'T WAIT

24. Come into Reality So Something New Can Happen

> I must be capable of looking at you,
> not through barriers, screens of my prejudices and conditioning.
> I must be in communion with you,
> which means I must love you.
>
> —J. KRISHNAMURTI, THE BOOK OF LIFE

Seeing clearly in reality helps us make wise choices. We're right here in present time, seeing people and situations as they are without superimposing past images, expectations, or interpretations. Reality includes seeing a situation from many sides so you can make reasoned decisions based on the whole picture, not just a fragment of reality. It's like walking out of a very limited, murky space into a clear sunny day and looking in all directions.

Building on all that has come before—an awareness of our stuck places, an ability to deeply attune to ourselves and the world around us, showing up as we are—we become better able to shed our illusions, images, and expectations, and stand right here in present time. To live in reality is to take the fear out of our hearts, the blinders off our eyes, the censors out of our minds, and the mufflers off our ears and see the whole picture of life with its many shades and colors—from beauty, joy, and love, to suffering, pain, and cruelty. It's there, it's the "what is" of life. To live in reality is to see the "what is" of a situation without making interpretations that take us into our head and away from experience. If it's cold and rainy, instead of saying, "It's a nasty day," you simply say, "It's cold and rainy." (Having lived through two recent fire seasons brought home how much this is all relative. How we longed for a cold rainy day.) If a child is smiling at herself in the mirror, you don't say, "Oh she loves looking at herself," you say, "She's smiling at herself in the mirror." That's all you really know. The rest is an interpretation coming through your filter that takes you away from being completely in reality.

This may sound like a small thing, but when we move away from reality into interpretations, judgments, and conclusions, we move away from our deepest experience of life. You can experiment with this and see what it feels like to you. It's subtle but powerful.

To live in reality is also to allow ourselves to feel our emotions. If you have to wait two hours at the doctor's office, you're moving away from reality when you grit your teeth and say to yourself, "I shouldn't be upset. I don't want to seem like an angry person." The truth is that you are frustrated and angry and wish the hell they'd use more sense in scheduling appointments. This doesn't mean you need to scream at the office staff, but you don't have to bottle up your feelings either. You can feel them, then consider what would be respectful yet honest to say.

Living in reality helps you notice what you truly want and don't want. For example, let yourself know who you'd really like to invite over for dinner. No shoulds. No "that's not nice." Allow yourself to scan your list of friends and see who brings up a warm or happy feeling.

To live in reality is to realize that all the censors, critics, and saboteurs in your mind are relics from the past. Sometimes you move into reality by simply noticing your behavior. Here's an example: Although Mac loved music, he entered engineering school because engineering was a much higher status, higher money-making profession. After his first semester of getting nearly all As, his grades slowly dropped, largely because he was spending so much time in a jazz band and other musical groups. By his second year, the grades dropped further and his adviser asked him in to talk. He asked Mac, "Tell me about all the musical activities you're part of." After he heard the list, he said to Mac, "What is this telling you?" Forty years later, Mac is still waking up with joy to teach high school music.

When we live in reality we simply hear what people are saying without adding or subtracting any interpretations or meaning. We take note of those nagging feelings that say, "don't do it," or the bright feelings that say, "why not, it could be a great adventure." If someone is harming us, we don't make up excuses or reasons; we see the harm. Conversely, we also are open to the incredible care, beauty, kindness, and love that is all around us.

Being in reality helps us make wise decisions about jobs, relationships, and lifestyle changes, as well as all the little decisions that pepper our lives. We feel an internal resonator instead of a critic and censor. Rather than being confused by thoughts such as, "I don't deserve something so good," or "What will my parents think?" we ask "Is this job realistic for me, does it fit with my relationships, my goals, my desired lifestyle?" It feels much simpler.

Being in reality also opens the way to loving relationships. I'm here with you right now—not some image of what I want you to be, not some fearsome face from the past. I'm in a living, breathing, dynamic exchange with you that includes feelings, thoughts, and that undefinable experience beyond words. The center of our relationship is wanting to know who we are in this moment. Drawing on Krishnamurti's words, when we look at each other without the barriers and screens of our prejudices we come into true communion with each other—heart, mind, and spirit. This helps create a calming shelter for one another, whether it be in a primary relationship, with friends, or in a spiritual community.

Part of seeing clearly in the present involves seeing the past clearly too. Most families span the continuum from goodness to insensitivity, to neglect, to harm. For some it is heavily weighted at one end or the other. The first step is to recognize the conclusions you still hold from the distant past: people are dangerous. I am helpless. People are kind. I'm unlovable. I'm a loser. People won't like me if I have a strong opinion. It's not safe to love. The second step is to recognize those patterns of belief that feel so real, but not to be controlled by them. The third step is to come into present time and ask yourself, "What will help improve my life right now? How can I walk through these feelings of fear, uncertainty, or doubt and do something new, real, and true?"

Many people resist this exploration because it takes effort and a willingness to let go of long-held interpretations that feel "normal." This journey is about pulling the rug out from under all concepts of "how it is." I love the expression "it blows your mind." That's exactly what happens as we free ourselves—we let a fresh breeze sweep out the chambers of the mind so old thoughts disintegrate, leaving a spaciousness that allows something new to happen. We stop being glued to rigid, outdated beliefs.

Letting go in this way can feel unsettling and leave us wondering who we are. Our internal experience feels unfamiliar when we're not quite so tightly held together. Also, our emotional experience can change dramatically with unfamiliar feelings arising and falling in new rhythms. If we can just hang out with our experience and let ourselves be astonished and then changed, we will start getting unstuck in every part of our being. The willingness to be unsure, uncomfortable, and unknowing opens the road to freedom.

Many people fear strong feelings as if they were something ferocious, threatening, or too much to bear. When we were children this may have been true, but when we label feelings as bad, dangerous, and overwhelming as adults, we experience them as inner chaos, and our well-conditioned nervous system wants to jump into action to get away from them. We blame others or make up excuses and stories and explanations. "You made me feel this way." "It must have been a lesson for my growth." "It's providence." "It's my karma." "Everything happens for a reason." While these thoughts might be comforting, they take us out of reality and away from our actual experience. We make human connections through a deeply felt presence, not through thoughts.

People also keep on their rose-colored glasses because they are deeply afraid of seeing the truth. For example, many people believe that if their parents were cruel to them it means that as a child they really were unlovable, worthless, or bad. They also believe that if they acknowledge the cruelty of their parents or others, it follows that they should hate them or have nothing to do with them. Then they often believe that if they see the current truth—my relationship is lousy, I hate this job—they have to do something about it immediately, otherwise they are imperfect.

All three of these beliefs reflect fallacies that keep us stuck. If your parents were negligent or abusive, it means nothing about you—they were acting out of their past interpretations and filters. If you accept that your parents were harmful, unskillful, and insensitive, you can experience your rage and sorrow and grief about it without hating them.

If you allow yourself to see the reality of a troubled relationship or job, you can move to action: talk about it, get help, or decide to stay for a while and create a survival plan. Avoid the formulas for how you should react in a given situation; there's no one way. The answers lie within your body—from noticing your sensations, to your energy level, to what rings right, clear, and true for you.

To make room for something new to happen in your life is to see without filters. You can ignite the spark of fresh ideas and aliveness within your body when you step out of the shadow of the past. You take off a veil of tired old reactions and patterns and step into the reality of the moment. It might be to see unhappiness; it might be to see a new possibility or realize someone cares about you. It will definitely broaden your view and free you to experience awe and wonder at this incredible universe.

25. Notice the Stories You Tell Yourself

You can't heal a story.
—STEPHEN WOLINSKY

Buddhism teaches us to be aware of the stories we tell ourselves. Stories are usually about the past or center around wishful thinking. They take us into our heads and stop us from being in our current experience with our feelings and emotions. It's like commenting on life rather than living it.

Because is a common word in many stories. "I can't swim *because* someone scared me when I was a child." "I don't push myself *because* I didn't want to outshine my family." "I can't lose weight *because* I'm afraid of intimacy." The internal response to such statements could well be, "How do you know! What have you tried?"

Another kind of story is talking about how we'd like life to be, rather than how it is. *Shoulds* and *I want* are common in these stories. "I don't think this relationship *should* be so hard. I *want* us to be relaxed and not get upset with each other. It's silly that we fight so much." But the truth is, if you are fighting and the relationship is difficult, you need to say so and acknowledge the pain before anything can change. You need to move into current time—fear, anxiety, and all—and say what's in your heart, what has you worried, what you are scared about. When you relate at this level you will be much closer to experiencing yourself and engaging in a real way with the other person. It is only from this place that relationships can change.

Similarly, if you are afraid of doing something, for example, swimming, drop the story and take action. Walk to the water's edge with a swimming teacher or a friend and take a step into the water, then another, then another, anxiety and all. Or admit to yourself you're really stumped about losing weight, and realize you need help.

Simply said, we drop the story and come into the whole truth of the present moment with all our feelings, fears, and experience. This frees us to move to a next step rather than staying locked into a tired old story that's either a fantasy or about past time.

You can also notice how your stories can stop you from feeling joy or happiness. Many people get scared at the fullness and expansiveness of joy and try to push it away by jumping out of the experience and into a story. Instead of feeling awe at a glorious sunset, they distance themselves with a torrent of words or, even more removed, they bring up some problem they are having, or suddenly say, "Time to go now." Any form of strong energy, be it joy or sorrow, has the potential to shake loose parts of us that are hiding. It's like a big wind blowing through us. To get unstuck is to invite the wind in.

One way I work with couples to get out of the story and into their connection is to have them face each other holding on to the end of a cord while keeping gentle eye contact and attuning to the other's breathing until they are breathing in the same rhythm. This often relaxes people and brings out tears or smiles and a sense of connection. It can also be scary, and one person might want to pull away. "Why are we doing this? We came here for therapy." But it is being in the experience together that often leads to a deepening of connection, to bringing on tenderness and ease.

When Martin Luther King, Jr., said that "unconditional love will have the final word in reality," he touched on a basic truth: that beneath our conditioning, defenses, and denial, love binds us together, and that is the ultimate reality. But we first have to relinquish our coverings to get there. Our daily practice is to notice our stories and hiding places, then dare to ease into silence, stillness, and our physical bodies, and experience what arises.

26. Play with the Kaleidoscope of Perception

Something has happened
To my understanding of existence
That now makes my heart always full of wonder
And kindness.

—HAFIZ, *THE GIFT*

I magine five photographers all standing at the top of the same mountain taking photos in all directions. All their pictures would be different because the photographers would literally be looking through different lenses—both their own eyes and the eye of their cameras—and with different levels of light exposure. Is one picture more true than another? No, they are all true. Reality is elusive. Just as you see many colors when light reflects on a prism, there are often many right outcomes to a situation.

When we decide to paint a house, we walk around the whole house to assess the extent of the project—we don't just look at the front and make an estimate. We notice the overhang, the decks, the number of windows, and the extra detail. It's not just a matter of square feet; it's about time, energy, difficulty, and number of coats of paint, as well as the weather forecast. To be unstuck, we do well to circle any situation or problem and ask: what are all the factors and possibilities and ways to perceive the situation?

Our concept that the sun rises is an illusion because the sun is still and we increasingly see it on the horizon as the earth turns toward the east. To play with this idea, the next time you watch the "sun rise" shift your focus and imagine yourself sitting on the earth as it turns toward the east with the sun coming into view. You can do the reverse with a sunset. The deeper purpose of this exploration is to get in the habit of rattling your mind and always entertaining the idea that a different perspective exists, possibly one beyond your comprehension. To get beyond your stuck places you repeatedly ask, "Is there some bigger truth beyond my grasp that I am unable to see from where I'm 'standing'?"

Society's perceptions of the physical world have been changing dramatically since the end of the Dark Ages. We've moved from believing the earth is flat or the sun moves around the earth to Newton's mechanical interpretation, to the subatomic world of waves, particles, relationships, and potentialities. Just as so-called scientific facts have been shattered and left by the wayside over and over again, superstitious beliefs have repeatedly given way to scientific discovery.

For example, at one time people believed that if lightning struck a house and burned it down it was God's retribution for some evil deed. Once Benjamin Franklin explored the phenomenon of lightning and created the lightning rod, those false beliefs were quickly dispelled. To live in reality is to ask ourselves, "Is this belief superstition, magical thinking, or based in reality?"

Part of learning to see the reality of a situation is to see it from the perspective of other people involved. In a riveting lecture by Pakistani journalist Amid Rashid, commenting on media coverage of the United States' invasion of Iraq in March 2003, he said, "What you see on TV here in America and what everyone else in the world sees, especially in the Middle East, are like night and day—completely different." If you are watching the news, being taught a theory or concept, ask yourself, "Who wrote the theory? What was omitted? Who benefits by it? Who is left out or harmed? Is there self-interest beneath the rhetoric?"

While I was driving along Route 12 from Lolo, Montana, to Idaho, once the path of the original Lewis and Clark trail, I stopped to read many of the historic signs describing and honoring their journey. The graffiti told a different story, largely from a Native American perspective—it referred to the trip as mapping the northwest to appropriate the land and commit genocide on Native Americans. It all depends whose shoes you are standing in.

To be unstuck is to have a wary eye for impassioned speeches, trixters, and culture-bound beliefs and customs, even right at home. Think of shifts of belief with regard to medicine, education, and health, for example, in your own lifetime. When I grew up it was customary to put iodine on cuts, which painfully burned the skin. Babies were not to be held "too much" or fed on demand—every four hours was the rule—because it would "spoil" them. Today, with our better understanding of infant attachment, we encourage what women have known for centuries—we feed babies when they are hungry and hold them as much as they need to feel secure.

We bring our perceptual field to relationships as well. Sometimes when we perceive another person as angry or disapproving, we've attributed our feelings to them. At a Ken Keyes training, whenever we had a critical perception of another person we were taught to first ask ourselves, "Am I talking about myself?" One woman in an interview said, "I was sure that a certain woman in our church group was angry at me because of a conversation we had had. I'd find myself looking away from her, having a knot in my gut every time I saw her. After feeling upset about it for a year, I asked her if she was angry at me, and she didn't even remember our little talk. She gave me a big smile and said she had been preoccupied." We can always check out a situation to see if we're misreading it.

I worked with a couple in which one partner kept insisting the other was angry. But, with exploration, it turned out that the stony face was about fear. The moral of the story: circle the situation, leave room for doubt, listen to others, put your feet in someone else's shoes, then come to a possible conclusion . . . and be willing to change it!

27. Explore Your History of Truth and Deception

The little fleeting glimpses that I have been able to have of truth can hardly convey an idea of the indescribable lustre of truth, a million times more intense than that of the sun.

—MAHATMA GANDHI

Telling the truth is the sister of being in reality. Being truthful starts by listening within, then speaking honestly without gauging the reactions of others. Truth winds its way through our lives at many levels: from telling the truth about the facts of our daily existence—where we went, what we ate, how much we spent—to knowing what we are feeling and thinking, to understanding our motivations and reactions, to following our deepest leadings about our lives, to eventually finding out that at our essence we are one with the energy of the whole universe. Yet the truth is often very difficult.

Many people distort truth to gain approval, impress people, cover their shame, or avoid getting in trouble. Deception is often a bad habit that was modeled by our parents. We say we're fine when we feel lousy. We say we don't need help when we do. We dramatize a story to get sympathy. In other words, we get short-term gains but sustain long-term losses of integrity.

Not being truthful reflects fear and a lack of inner awareness, attunement to physical sensations, emotions, and self-acceptance. Indeed, being truthful is tantamount to self-acceptance. If I tell you who I am without exaggerating or diminishing anything, I am fully present to you. I am not ashamed, afraid, or needing to "buy" the relationship in any way.

Living close to the bones of truth is grounding, connecting, and relaxing—there aren't any deceptions to catch up with us later. It may help to remember that while initially it may be scary to tell the truth, especially if you've been holding something back, with time truthfulness dispels fear—and makes room for love.

Scan your life history for vignettes or situations that relate to truth or dishonesty in your past. Are there scars from the deceptions and lies of others? Are there warm moments of remembering people you could count on to be honest and real with you? How did these experiences shape you as a child? As an adult? Here are some accounts that may bring back some of your own memories and feelings.

The Peroxide Story

Amy's mother, who often stressed honesty to her children, would use peroxide to clean out cuts or bruises. She would say, "Now if you cry, it won't bubble up and do its job." Believing her mother, Amy repeatedly stifled her tears when she got the peroxide treatment. Then one day, her brother took a nasty tumble off his bike and rushed into the house howling in pain. When their mother poured peroxide over the bruises, Amy felt alarmed when her brother kept crying and wanted to yell, "Stop crying or the peroxide won't bubble." To her astonishment, he continued crying and the peroxide *did* bubble. Amy watched in disbelief, feeling horrified: "She lied! It doesn't matter if you cry." This seemingly small event shattered Amy's sense of trust with her mother. "Why did she do that? What else is she lying about? Do I tell my brother and sister that our mother lies?"

Trying to Fit In by Exaggerating the Truth

Andrea's story: "As a young child in school I often made up or exaggerated stories to get attention or to impress people in the hope they would like me. In class when the teacher asked us to say how many states in the union we'd visited, I said thirty-eight when it was really thirty-one—I wanted to have visited more states than anybody else. I'd understate what I'd paid for something—it was really a good buy. Later I would monitor my words to help me fit in, please someone, or do the 'right' thing. I'd even pray, 'Please God help me say the right thing at the right time.' I realized later that my chronic dishonesty came out of deep feelings of being unlovable and not fitting in. A life change came about when I made a complete commitment to be truthful."

Fear of Conflict

"My greatest fear was having someone angry at me, so I avoided conflict as if it were a fatal disease. I'd say 'I'm fine' when I was sad, or 'It doesn't matter,' when someone hurt me, and I never told my husband how desperately lonely I was in our marriage. In close relationships I gave off mixed signals—I'd act friendly and do a lot of things for people but never talk about the turmoil underneath. I'd feel hurt or upset when they didn't reciprocate. I was bewildered and sad when I felt someone pulling away but never said anything—I'd just have this numbing kind of hurt.

"I was chronically indirect and would make hints or ask questions to get my way. Instead of saying, 'I'd like to go to the zoo,' I'd ask my husband, 'Don't you think it would be good to take the kids to the zoo?' My hinting and cajoling made people angry and impatient with me. 'Just tell me what you want!' my husband would practically scream at me. With a huge commitment and lot of work, I've finally found that place in me that knows what I want and then has the courage to say it. At first I feared being told I was arrogant and demanding, but over time my fear was proven false—at least most of the time—and my relationships are much better."

Denying a Child's Reality

Another woman, Leah, recounted, "My mother would agree to let me go to the movies. I'd bring it up to her in front of my father—'Can I go to the movies now?' And if he said, 'Shouldn't you stay home and help around the house?' my mother would say, 'I never told you you could go.' I would argue and plead—'But you said I could go!' and she'd repeat that she never said such a thing. I'd feel utterly hysterical inside—totally abandoned and alone. To this day when someone lies to me I can feel that place in my chest start to fire up and I want to convince them that they're lying. I vowed I would never lie to my children. It was such a horrible feeling."

Can you remember similar feelings and situations and how they played themselves out in your life? Were the distortions of truth subtle or blatant? Did you vow to be different, or do you find yourself doing exactly what was done to you, or a mixture of both? Gandhi's words—there is an indescribable luster of truth, more intense than that of the sun—applies so profoundly to every aspect of our lives.

Imagine taking off all the deceptions and distortions as if they were a cloak around you, being completely clear and honest and giving up control of the outcome of situations. How does it feel? Scary? Relieving? What comes to mind? Shedding the skin of deception is a courageous step in the journey of becoming unstuck. It brings a clarity and freedom to the flow of your inner world. Nothing left to hide, no fear of your past catching up to you!

What a blessing to keep company with another person who is deeply honest—to trust that he or she will say if they are upset, keep agreements, own their part in a situation, talk openly about their lives, admit to mistakes, and be kind. To be immaculate in living and telling the truth is to feel the luster of integrity shining in our lives. It takes us home to the best part of ourselves and brings us into profound connection with our brothers and sisters on the journey.

EXERCISE:

Explore Your Experiences with Truth and Deception

1. What is your history related to truth and deception? Have you been deceived in overt and covert ways? As a child? As an adult? How did you feel as a result? What effects does it have on your life?

2. Think of someone you can count on to be truthful in a kind way. What is it like being with that person?

3. What are ways in which you are dishonest, either by commission or omission, or by exaggerating? What underlies this? Fear, insecurity, wanting to be liked?

4. Think of what it would take to be more honest. (Aware of your feelings, more secure, not worried about what others think, willing to reveal yourself.)

5. Who are the people you are most honest with? What makes it easy to be open with them? What makes it more difficult with others?

28. Start Telling Your Truths, One Level at a Time

Lovers of wisdom must open their minds to very many things indeed.
—HERACLITUS

Truths are seldom fixed. We could talk about your truth as your perspective in the moment, or what feels right for you. To free yourself by telling your truths means to attune deeply to the emotions and thoughts that come from your core, and to reveal them. It keeps your interior world flowing and open rather than restricted or congested. The concept of living by our truths permeates life in many ways, but if you can focus on some basics, you will have a clear way to begin.

The first level of truth telling is simply stating facts without exaggerating, subtracting, embroidering, or distorting them.

Gary, forty-eight, spoke in an interview about his troubled childhood, his absent, raging father, subsequent contentious relationships, and a marriage strewn with affairs, broken agreements, deception, hanging on, and eventual divorce. He spoke of repeating the patterns of his father with his own sons: I didn't listen to them, play catch, or take them fishing.

As we were coming to the end of our time together, having revealed a life filled with regret and sadness, he said, in a heartfelt way, his eyes shining with tears, "I just want to be honest. I don't want to hurt anyone anymore, and I don't want to feel guilty."

I asked, "What does that mean in your everyday life?"

Gary replied, "It means to tell the truth. Not to exaggerate when I speak—not say we caught a zillion fish when that's nonsense. We caught four. Not to say I earned five thousand dollars this month when I earned three. I want to keep agreements, be timely in paying bills, be proud of what I do, honest in my relationships."

The truth expressed in this simple way is the starting place for many people. Not stretching, fudging, avoiding, or omitting anything. Just say how much you spent, how many chocolates you ate, how many (or few) miles you went on the treadmill, whether or not you made the difficult phone call, how much you like a poem you wrote, how someone hurt your feelings. No more, no less, no complicated stories.

The second level of living in truth is telling the truth about our inner experience, which has to do with being clear about our feelings. This requires a deeper awareness of ourselves—both our body sensations and our feelings. I can't tell my friend or partner that I'm sad unless I feel my sadness. I might need to start by recognizing the symptoms of sadness—a tight chest, a knot in the throat, a sensation around my eyes—rather than the actual feelings. Our journey of becoming unstuck is truly a journey of connecting with body sensations, emotions, and feelings. We also need to recognize that we may be hiding a core feeling under other feelings. For example, many people cover hurt with anger, while others camouflage anger with sadness or helpless crying.

The third level of knowing our truth is exploring our motivation.

We need to reflect and ask, will my words do harm? Are they coming out of a sense of caring or out of veiled anger or a desire to hurt? Once we discern the difference, we need to restrain ourselves from the well-placed dig or the hurtful remark.

Being aware of your motivation will help you see the parts of you that are lonely or hurt or want power. For example, you may find that gossiping about another person's failings or gloating over someone's misfortunes reflects an insecurity—perhaps you're trying to make yourself feel important. If you're willing to look at your insecurity instead of gossiping, you can make friends with your insecure place. It doesn't mean one never talks about anyone. A teacher who tells a parable or story to educate has a far different motivation.

The fourth level of living in the truth is when you separate the past from the present. Usually sudden shots of anger, raging at others, feeling hurt, or impulses to run away are reactions that stem from the past. If it's an old reaction being triggered it's helpful to take a few moments to come back to current time and ask, "What was actually said or done? Is there a common pattern to my reaction? What's it really about? What meaning did I attribute to the situation?"

Ella, who had worked to separate her "nervous system" reactions from current situations, came to a recent session with her husband, eyes shining, voice animated. "I can't wait to tell you what happened.

There I was going off at him, like I often do, but it was like it was happening over there, and I was sitting here looking at it, and thinking, 'Why am I doing that? I love him.'" She paused, then continued. "It was almost as if someone else was saying those things."

This marvelous moment was a huge departure from her typical righteous ranting at her partner and her belief that he truly was the bad guy. She had seen her conditioned self as separate from her essence, or observing "I." Her husband, on hearing her account, looked at her wide-eyed, surprised, and relieved. "I see you differently," he said, astonished. They both could step back and observe the ranting as not the deepest truth. That she loved him was much closer to the heart of reality. It softened their relationship.

Truth, Kindness, and Right Timing

What use is there in a blunt truth thrown like a stone, which breaks the heart? There is no virtue in truth which has no beauty.
—HIDAYAT INAYAT-KHAN, SUFI TEACHER

Telling the truth is not to be confused with blurting out anything that comes to mind, venting anger, or telling someone's secrets under the guise of, "I thought you ought to know," or an innocent, "I was just telling the truth." I love Inayat-Khan's words, "There is no virtue in truth which has no beauty." Likewise, there is no beauty in words that are intended to undermine, wound, shame, or harm.

Mindfulness, kindness, and truth need to merge as one. This doesn't mean that a partner might not be sad or upset when we tell them we're leaving, but it's far different to say the truth without the intent to harm than to make a verbal stab at someone. There is music in our words when they come from a kind heart and mind. A deep part of a spiritual practice is to drop back inside and speak with intent to be clear, true, and kind.

When we start committing to tell the truth, we often feel two parts of ourselves arguing inside: the part that wants to edit or exaggerate, which rises up to vie with the other part that has committed to being honest. If it is difficult to relinquish coloring your stories, ask yourself, "What is this about? What will I feel if I tell the unadorned truth? Why am I doing this? What would happen if I simply told the truth?" Then dare to do it, and see what happens.

Guidelines

1. Make a vow to yourself to be completely honest about the facts of your life. Notice what you are seeking in conversations when you want to exaggerate or minimize a story. What happens when you resist the temptation and just tell the truth?

2. Notice the body sensations that go with truth or deception. (In the beginning, you actually may feel more uneasy with the truth.)

3. Make a commitment not to talk about anyone negatively behind their back. Get clear about your concern and go directly to the person involved.

4. When in doubt about whether to say something, don't say it. Even a minute of uneasiness or a wiggle of doubt suggests you are not clear. Take time to think about what you want to say. Discern your motivation. It's a challenge to realize that your perceptions are the result of your lens and can be a limited view of reality.

29. Take Off the Lenses That Color Your Truth

Lenses can be thought of as the particular focus we use to interpret the world. They can be dark or rose colored. Common

lenses are worry, fear, suspicion, or a belief that the world is dangerous, you can't trust anyone, or you must be perfect to be accepted.
On the other extreme we have filters such as, "Everything will take
care of itself," "Everyone is really good," or "I can do anything I set
my mind to." Both sides of the spectrum give us an incomplete picture of the world.

People are adept at defending their lenses because they seem so
familiar and real. A parent might retort, "What do you mean I worry
too much about my children? It's natural to worry about your kids.
All parents do." We need to question our assumptions about what's
natural and realize that what's natural to us isn't necessarily natural
to others. It usually has more to do with our conditioning than any
law of nature. Challenging our filters can be like popping the bub-
bles we live in or being shaken to our core.

When you take off a lens or filter you can see more of life's grada-
tions and ambiguities. This demands your presence in the moment.
Being free of lenses can be compared to being in a sailboat in which
safety requires that you notice the changing winds, clouds, and
waves, and that you react appropriately. There is no rule book to follow. Even though you've studied or gone to sailing classes, survival
depends on awareness in current time.

Living without lenses makes life relatively quiet because you are
not so busy rationalizing, and you're not having exhausting internal
arguments trying to fit people and events into your limited box. At
first the quiet of reality may seem dry and boring in contrast with
the drama and chaos of running from the truth. But with time, you
settle into a vast stillness like "the peace that passeth understanding."

It can be uncomfortable to be around a group of people whose
lenses are different from yours. For example, if you see through the
theistic lens of Christianity, you might feel uneasy around someone
who sees through the lens of Buddhism, which has no concept of
God. Many people find it extremely challenging to accept that most
"beliefs" are lenses, not necessarily truths. People debate their lenses—

it's true or not true—they fight over them and hate over them because the ego thinks lenses are real. But just as anyone can take off their glasses, consider dropping your most cherished lens for a moment and see how it feels.

If you drop into stillness and follow that quiet stream of what feels clear and right, a steadiness and power grows within you. When you live close to the truth as it arises moment to moment, you are in the flow of your being—a place where words and opinions fall away.

30. Commit to Living by the Truth— Fear and All

If we value reality and truth as we value sunshine, clean air, and clear water, we might realize it is the breath of life. It's one with our integrity, joy, health, relationships, and stability.

In our journey to truth, we start having deeper conversations that simultaneously can be relieving and anxiety-provoking because our secrets, hiding places, and devious thoughts will be exposed. Coming into reality and feeling the incredible luster of truth means stepping beyond the grip of fear over and over again. You take action, fear and all. You say what's true, fear and all. Ultimately you risk losing everything but yourself and your connection to the flow of life. Once you truly experience that anything but the truth hurts inside— it creates uneasiness, tightness, dullness, a nagging feeling—you become all the more motivated to get to the truth as quickly as possible and allow the internal sunshine and soft breezes to return.

Being real with people does run the risk of evoking strong feelings or conflict and can sometimes lead to loss. It also has the potential to deepen understanding, draw you closer together, and change the direction of a relationship. I have seen snarly relationships improve dramatically when the protected heart is revealed and the tears start to flow. Some people are relieved when secrets are brought to light—like being able to get out of a private prison by having a friend who understands. "You don't think I'm disgusting and terrible for what I've done?" "No, I'm glad you told me. I feel trusted." Our connection grows stronger, we drop into silence together, and there is more love available than we ever could have dreamed of.

Once we commit to living in reality and telling the truth as best we can, life becomes simple. Not easy, but simple. Instead of second guessing our responses, we listen internally and reveal whatever arises—again with kindness, right timing, and appropriateness. We realize it is our task to accept the outcome, even if it is very difficult because being at one with reality and truth is at the heart of our commitment to live with integrity.

This is June's account of waking up to what it means to tell the truth: "I had a terribly hard time telling people the truth, but I wouldn't have called it that. I would have said I wanted to say the right thing or please others or not create conflict. I was completely afraid to express anger, but often my words would come out sideways or like little digs. Then on a camping trip with a friend and her daughter, we got into a hot situation and I dropped the 'nice' facade and started to cry. 'What should I have said?' I asked my friend. 'Just say the truth!' she shouted in frustration. 'Say what's true—what you like or want or feel . . . and let the chips fall where they may!' I was stunned. It was like waking up to a burst of bright energy. 'Oh, that's all I have to do. Just say what's going on with me. No guessing, wondering, anticipating, just let it all happen.' My life was forever changed."

Committing to living by the truth is similar to saying, "I will not live in fear," because fear is the prime motivator for distorting the truth. I'm afraid you won't like me so I'll flatter you. I'm afraid I'm inadequate so I'll work seventy hours a week and prove I'm successful. When you can say to yourself, "Let it all fall apart, let me be alone, disliked, broke, but I will not live in fear, I will not tolerate this knot in my gut, this tight body or racing thoughts," you are free. Returning to Gandhi's words, we remember that "there is an indescribable lustre to the truth."

31. My Truth, Thy Truth: We Are Part of a Web

In *Experiments with Truth*, Mahatma Gandhi wrote that *ahimsa* is based on the search for the truth and that "a perfect vision of truth can only follow a complete realization of *ahimsa*." Ahimsa refers to the underlying unity of all life.

> It is quite proper to resist and attack a system, but to resist and
> attack its author is tantamount to resisting and attacking oneself.
> For we are all tarred with the same brush, and are children of one
> and the same Creator, and as such the divine powers within us are
> infinite. To slight a single human being is to slight those divine
> powers, and thus to harm not only that being but with him the
> whole world.
>
> —MAHATMA GANDHI

To be unstuck is to broaden our vision and live by the greater truths—to feel our relationship to all people and all sentient life. In Gandhi's words, we are children of one and the same creator. To harm another is to harm ourself. I would add to love others is to feel love inside.

The only way we stay fully in reality is to see and accept our connection to the reality of the whole. This will involve a level of listening and attuning that takes us far beyond our conditioned self. You start by realizing that you *don't know* another person's experience, nor can you generalize from your own history. From my own childhood experiences, I can't know what it's like to grow up as an African American, or a person in poverty, or in a family where people feel depressed and helpless.

The crucial thing to remember is this: *while we can't know another person's experience, we can listen with the heartfelt intent of understanding. Such listening becomes the pathway to human communion. This nourishes us at all levels because it assuages feelings of separation.* This requires a deep ability to stay present to strong feelings and not run away with defensiveness, not wanting to counter what other people are saying.

I have attended numerous workshops on race, class, homophobia, Native American culture, and the like. There is utter magic when people open themselves to understand one another. At the 1985 conference for the International Decade of Women in Nairobi, Kenya, I sat through a workshop listening to African American women voice their anger at the inequities and pain they've experienced and how they felt let down by feminists and feminism with its white, middle-class origins. I could feel my ego murmuring a feeble but, but . . . what about . . . ? Mostly, I felt stunned into silence. I realized the best way to show respect and caring was to be completely present to the anger, to feel it along with the accumulated pain and hurt that lay just below the surface. In another workshop a woman from Palestine engaged in a heated dialogue with an Israeli woman. Tempers flared between them and within the audience, but it was riveting—at least there was an intent to hear, to form some kind of bridge.

Some people are uneasy hearing about the differences in other people's experience and immediately rush to talk about how we're all essentially alike. That's our conditioned, ego-self afraid of being disturbed. We want a pretty picture. It's hard to be present to accounts of poverty, violence, injustice, abuse, and alienation. Yes, there are human commonalties, but it's absolutely crucial that we first hear people speak of their pain, customs, anger, and joy; to listen deeply and be touched by their lives and experiences and how they have suffered from the inequities of the system.

At a training on homophobia that I led for therapists I was deeply moved by the humble attention of the male and female heterosexual counselors as two lesbian women and a gay man spoke of their negative and positive experiences with counselors. The therapists were open-minded and willing to be shaken, which they were, because they thought there was nothing much they needed to learn, they were operating with the common conception, "we're all people." They were astounded to realize the extent of their lack of understanding of homophobia. The experience of the training was positive because of the profound respect and everyone's willingness to be known, albeit in different ways. The therapists exposed their lack of knowledge and the three people who told their stories had an opportunity to be heard with dignity and respect. They deeply appreciated the willingness of the therapists to learn from them.

There is no one reality in the amazing web of lives drawn together in the mosaic of humanity. There is everyone's experience. If you are willing to come to the table with all your brothers and sisters—rich, poor, Muslim, Jew, Buddhist, Christian, lesbian, heterosexual—you will go far deeper into yourself than through any book or lecture. To simply sit and listen with the intention of attuning to another person's world is to build the most important bridge we humans can ever cross. Knowing dissolves into caring, and caring dissolves into love. We create a shield against violence and tap into our humanity, where we find the seeds of generosity and care.

Once we're willing to recognize the differences, we will naturally experience the similarities. All people have families, we all suffer loss and have to cope with the looming reality of death. All people want to feel cared for, to be free of suffering, and to be happy. I end this section as I started it, with a quote from Martin Luther King, Jr.:

> I believe that unarmed truth and unconditional love will have the final word in reality.

Connect with Others, Connect with Life

32. Experience the Four Abodes of Loving Relationships

*And in the sweetness of friendship let
there be laughter and sharing of pleasures.
For in the dew of little things the heart
finds its morning and is refreshed.*

—KAHLIL GIBRAN, *THE PROPHET*

In Buddhism, the Four Divine Abodes, known as the Brahma Viharas or Four Noblest Qualities of Mind, can be related to the boundless, immeasurable, restorative qualities that lie at the heart of loving relationships. They are:

> *Loving kindness and friendliness,*
> *Compassion and empathy,*
> *Joy and rejoicing,*
> *Equanimity and peace of mind*

These qualities are at the heart of our ability to feel trust, love, ease, and peace of mind in all our relationships. Think of times when a comment or words of encouragement became a catalyst for change. Think of a time when you were able to take on a difficult situation, knowing you had an understanding friend or loved one cheering for you. Remember times when a kind word or gesture or friendliness and warmth of someone helped you get past feeling bad about yourself.

Think about community projects undertaken by various groups of people that helped improve the community or created resources for less advantaged people. Think of the themes or titles of popular songs that touch you in a special way: "You are my sunshine." "You're my everything." "I only live for the touch of your hand." "It's paradise to be near you." "Because of you my life is now worthwhile, and I can smile because of you." "When you go away it's a rainy day."

I used to think of these words as a lot of "codependent" drivel. Yet, I wondered, why do popular songs touch us so deeply that we listen to them over and over? Why do I often request "Someone to Watch Over Me," and feel myself melting inside, or feel my childhood camp song, "White wings, they never grow weary, they carry me tenderly over the sea"? Then it dawned on me that these are "attachment" songs. A mother's smile is like sunshine to a baby. Paradise is being tenderly held, comforted, and smiled at. A child literally comes into existence through being seen, and responded to. Without human connection children disconnect, start building walls, and in extreme cases can die. Our need for attachment and connection may shift with time, but that fundamental desire for bonding with a loving person is fully human and real and a lifelong need.

There is a paradox between the language of Buddhism and the language of Western psychology with regards to the concept of attachment. For Buddhists, attachment refers to clinging and demanding and is a source of our suffering. But attachment is used in psychology to describe a life-giving healthy relationship between a parent and child. In other words, we say a child is well bonded or attached to a parent. This means the child feels secure, cared for, at ease, and trusting that his or her needs will be met. It connotes the picture of a baby in the arms of a highly attuned parent—usually the mother—being adored and delighted in, exchanging smiles, coos, and making eye contact.

We often hear that as we mature we should be less dependent and more autonomous. I would say we need to be more skillful at cooperating, giving and receiving from each other, and learning how to be deeply connected to others while maintaining our own sense of self. Separation is the essential cause of anxiety, connection is the great healer. Supportive loving relationships are like good food: they give us the strength to take on challenges, heal emotional scars, or solve difficult problems.

In the journey of breaking free, it helps to become aware of how deeply intertwined we are with each other. Think back to times when someone was kind, loving, or especially friendly to you, particularly when you were in need. Notice how your body feels right now as you bring up the memories. I immediately feel a soothing warmth when I think of the encouraging words of a favorite piano teacher, or being snuggled up to Grandma while she read to me. We live in each other in a myriad of ways—body, mind, and spirit. Every moment of empathy, understanding, kindness, and encouragement that flows between us is like the milk and honey of human existence, softening our hearts, soothing our nervous systems, bridging our sense of separateness.

33. Create a Safe Shelter for Each Other

We can do together what we can never do alone. Relationships can help us laugh, gain perspective, and give us the impetus to stretch our wings and get unstuck.

Reach Out, Reach Back

The people I interviewed who generally stayed unstuck all knew how to ask for and receive help, cheer for each other, and have fun together. Many were part of a supportive community in which there were built-in channels for getting help; others had the resources of friends and family. Their comments often echoed Jesus of Nazareth's words: "When I was hungry, you fed me; . . . when I was naked, you clothed me; . . . when I was sick you visited me." (Matthew 25:35–36.) In other words, I was in need and you came to me. Feeling safe in life means you can reach out for help when you are in need and someone will reach back and take your hand.

In a training on attachment therapy with couples, Susan M. Johnson presented this scenario. "Imagine yourself in a long dark tunnel. A dragon is coming your way, getting closer and closer. You're backed against the wall: there's no where to run. What does it feel like?" How you survive in that tunnel depends on whether or not you have someone standing beside you, holding your hand, helping you take on the fearful dragon. She continued, "We're all up against the wall in that tunnel, facing the dragon of death."

When we can find rest and delight in each other, and take each other into our hearts, we open to a deep source of calming, healing, and joy. The following quotes reflect aspects of the Buddha's Four Divine Abodes of loving relationships: loving, kindness and friendliness, compassion and empathy, joy and rejoicing, equanimity and peace of mind.

"The day I finished a year-long project, I called some friends to meet me at a restaurant and celebrate. Twelve people showed up. What a joy!"

"I can count on my friend Pat to tell me when I'm getting off base—she never takes sides when I'm talking about my difficult relationship. She listens and tells me how she's acted like my partner and gives me insight into myself."

"I was wanting a new challenge and outlet when I turned fifty. A friend was willing to show me how to backpack in the mountains and take river canoe trips. She helped a fantasy become reality."

"My church group helped me with child care when I was ill."

"My husband surprised me on our anniversary with a weekend getaway at a cabin. He arranged child care and even packed my bags."

Let Loving Relationships Heal Trauma

Come unto me and I shall give you rest.
—JESUS OF NAZARETH

The power of supportive relationships is reflected in our growing understanding of the legacy of trauma. As Susan Johnson teaches, "Being isolated and alone when we are faced with unbearable pain, terror or torment is itself traumatic." When people recount sickness, assault, death of a loved one, or other trauma, it is the sense of being alone that leaves the indelible scar that can haunt one for life.

Conversely, one of the greatest predictors of healing from trauma is the ability to ask for and receive comfort and care. This reciprocal flow is more important than the nature and extent of past trauma. Authentic connections can take many forms: friendliness, helping, holding, listening, adventure, playing, celebrating, and humor. It takes courage to reach through old beliefs about not trusting people and risk making the connections, but it is key for everyone.

The concept of healthy attachment goes against the belief that you have to be "whole" to have a relationship and suggests that you become more whole through loving relationships, even when there is a history of trauma. Just like infants, our bodies relax and our internal systems organize and flow together when we are greeted with a smile, a warm hello, and outstretched arms. Just like infants, we too feel distressed and become internally disorganized when we are met with a blank face, criticism, or indifference. While as adults we have more internal resources to handle cold or troubling resources, we still are affected by them, especially when they persist over time.

If we have a secure base of care and support it lives within us on a daily basis. Conversely, when we perceive ourselves as cut off and alone, our bodies and mind will experience chronic stress and agitation. Martie spoke of a recent situation with her partner. "I was getting more and more agitated from the clutter and stacks of stuff around the house. Yesterday I was about to lose it. Instead of meeting my frantic state with criticism or disgust, my partner said kindly, 'Martie, what can I do for you?' She brought me coffee and toast, sat down beside me, hugged me and said, 'It's okay, I can help you. Where would you like to start?'" Tears shone in Martie's eyes as she talked. "That was so wonderful . . . not to be put down for how frantic I get. To be met with understanding. I could feel my whole body calming down. I felt so close to Judy—so loved."

Judy's response illustrates the Buddhist principle of loving kindness—meeting her beloved with understanding and care, instead of being caught up in her swirl of frustration or fear. When we can rest securely in our own world, and reach out into the tornado of other people's worries and dramas, without falling in, we become a source of healing.

Expanding our concept of connection, if we think of our relationships as one big relationship—that is, the way we walk in the world, with kindness, respect, and friendliness toward all—we will heal the fractures within us and between us. There is no hierarchy of human worth because it is all one life, one people, one water, one breath moving through time and space.

Come Together in Community

Sangha, one of the Three Jewels of Buddhism, means coming together as a community of like-minded people to know one another, give support, and do spiritual practices together. It can be as simple as gathering regularly at someone's home to meditate, have a discussion, and sit for tea. Any group in which you're getting to know one another, giving support, and deepening awareness can be sangha. Native American women traditionally made talking circles; my grandmother was a member of a book chat club for thirty years; consciousness-raising groups abounded in the late sixties. Recently, a woman at my

Quaker meeting announced she was starting a spiritual nurturing group—nearly all the women in the meeting signed up in spite of busy lives and full schedules. Many people find life-giving connections in peace and justice organizations or contributing to their community in some way.

When we have a flow of connections that provide care and support, we build up a reservoir of resilience, like money in the emotional bank that filters through our days and sustains us in difficult times. Just as children thrive with loving kindness from a caregiver, so too we are sustained by friendship, spiritual nurture, and a sense of belonging throughout our lives.

34. Mirror Mirror, Who Am I? Know Yourself Through Relationships

While relationships can be liberating, they can also become a quagmire. This is understandable because everything within us—conscious and unconscious—comes into play in close relationships. Our childhood fears of being abandoned, our neediness, our sense of entitlement, or the unspoken anger at our parents often comes flying to the surface. In other words, whatever has been stuck within us finds its way to the surface in relationships, especially in our more intimate relationships.

In this way, relationships are like mirrors constantly reflecting, affecting, and permeating our being. We meet our dragons and celebrate our gifts in a relationship. We see our shame through the secrets we keep, our fears in the lies we tell, our anger in the ways we become impatient, break agreements, hold back, or seduce others. We experience our generosity when we forget ourselves and care for another, our steadfastness when we stay connected through conflict, our tenderness in grieving with a friend, our playfulness in a shared adventure.

It's kind of like the old carnival funhouse mirrors that distort your image. Some mirrors make you tall, others fat, all change your shape. We often feel very different around different people because everyone is a different mirror.

What does the mirror teach me? If I suddenly feel afraid around someone, am I picking up their fear or tapping into mine, or both? This can require some sorting out. If you are usually relaxed around people but have a sudden flash of fear around a particular person it might signal you are attuning to something that's being hidden, or possibly anger that lies just beneath the surface that might erupt if you press their limits or challenge their story line. It's different matter if you are afraid of nearly everyone—in that case, you need to notice thoughts that jump to mind automatically when you're interacting with others.

Getting close to the mirror may also penetrate our hearts and bring forth tenderness, strength, and kindness we didn't know we had. We have a sudden urge to bring flowers to a friend who is suffering, to create something to amuse her; to sing a song, read a poem, or voice our appreciation and delight in knowing him. We soften inside when our beloved looks at us tenderly, eyes glistening, and says, "You mean so much to me." In return we soften and feel that tender spot in our hearts that had once grown cold.

We hear a great deal about how much we learn through suffering, but I believe we learn even more through love because it frees the heart. When people love us more than we believe we deserve, we get scared or thrown off center. How can this be, how can I receive this? I'm so undeserving. But if for a moment we allow the care and tenderness of another to soak deep into our being, we might feel a small crack in the shield around our heart. As the protective barrier dissolves, we feel our tears along with our joy. Kindness and care have an immense power to transform and heal.

35. Find the Wisdom That Flows Between Your Heart and Mind

The head is capable of amassing knowledge and information, but when the head, body, and heart become attuned and flow together we find wisdom. This provides a resource for making decisions that goes beyond the intelligence of the mind alone. This flow from head to heart extends to the rest of the body so we are operating as a congruent whole, a being instead of fragmented parts. Candace Pert, in *Molecules of Emotions*, writes about being attuned to the incredible web of receptors throughout the body: "We gain a sense of being rooted, steady, able to trust our perceptions and make wise decisions. Our perceptual field expands tremendously. Our decisions are supported by love, kindness, concern for others, mindfulness of the long-term effects on people and the environment." Over the years I've led numerous guided imageries into the heart in which people breathe into the heart area. Some people describe their experience as a sensation of the heart encased in a shell with wires around it, gray and lifeless, or covered with scar tissue. At the other end of the spectrum, others describe a softness, warmth, and ease, especially as they are grieving their losses and becoming more merciful with themselves. Other people feel nothing at all—the area around the heart feels disconnected and remote.

On your journey of getting unstuck and becoming free you need to soften the barriers around your heart. If you imagine how your unfinished grief, hurt, anger, and bitterness is creating holding patterns in your heart—dense, constricted, strained—it's easy to understand how these feelings keep you from being able to love fully, create, make changes, or have full access to your wisdom. When you allow your grief and sorrow to be felt, a tremendous softening occurs and love becomes a natural state of being. You act and react in tune with your natural self, which is in an unaffected state of love and compassion. You naturally go beyond the common dualities of I and other—I need you, I own you, I want you. It's the difference between doing life and being life.

To soften your heart, bring your awareness to the daily experiences in which you hold back, break agreements, feel ill at ease, want to run away, get defensive or anxious, or resist being present with your feelings. What would happen if instead of shutting down or running away you ease into your feelings and body sensations? You can remember that feelings are simply energy passing through you; they are all Buddha energy—Buddha being angry, Buddha being hurt, Buddha being deceptive, Buddha being joyful. There is nothing that is not Buddha energy, thus there is nothing to run from or label as bad or dangerous. And as you make friends with all parts of yourself, you will feel greater flow and ease in your body.

> *The mystics are relaxed at all times. When you lose your ease, you can say, "I'm so happy you brought this to my attention. This is really throwing me off. I'm not relaxed. I need to notice this deeply."*
> —SHABDA KAHN, SUFI TEACHER

EXERCISE:

Exercises to Open the Heart

Don't be discouraged if this takes time—the way of a peaceful heart is our life's journey.

1. *Softening the heart.* Soften your belly, drop your shoulders, and breathe into the area around your heart. Imagine a relaxing, soothing, comforting energy coming down through your head,

going through your neck and into your whole chest area, bringing even more energy into your heart. Stay with this for a while, continuing to focus on your heart.

2. *Make friends with your protective walls.* If you imagine a protective wall around your heart, touch it, feel it, be with it. Don't try to tear it down; just get to know it. Be kind to it, and notice any memories or feelings that arise. Visit it often.

3. *Play music or songs that bring joy to your heart.*

4. *Experiment with images of your heart as being cleared of all the obstructions, tension, and scars.* Some people image streams of light energy, flowing water, friends helping and scrubbing, or being rocked tenderly in loving arms in a room bathed with a gentle light.

36. Be Wise About Lovers and Friendships

Part of living in reality is having the wisdom to pick out friends and lovers with whom you have a flow and a feeling of mutuality. Sometimes friendships are instantaneous, similar to falling in love, we meet a kindred spirit and feel a strong liking that continues for years. Sometimes those instantaneous feelings can mislead us. Other times friendships evolve over time.

You can't *make* a friendship happen. Friendships are gifts that evolve with their own flow, rhythm, and pace. You can help them along by reciprocating and doing your part, but the magnetism happens at its own level. Even so, we need to modulate our instant attractions to others with wisdom from our past.

Here's a basic premise for developing friendships that help you stay unstuck: go toward people who are reliable, responsive, interested in knowing you, and supportive of your best self. Do not repeatedly put your energy into people who are indifferent, unreliable, and unresponsive to you. Remember to switch it around and consider that if you want solid friendships you also need to be reliable and responsive to those you would like to spend time with.

Another aspect of pleasurable relationships is the willingness to reveal yourself; that is, talk about both your rough and smooth spots. Some people find this scary—they tell themselves, "If I'm myself she might not like me." That may be true, but think of the experience as collecting data. You're finding out whether or not a person can be real with you, handle differences, and support your best self. If you are a tender, poetic soul and present yourself as Mr. Strong Success, then what happens when the mask falls off? Truth in packaging is a much better approach. Be your tender self, bring a rose, tell her you're anxious, and see what happens. This is the only way to create an I-Thou rather than an I-Other relationship.

It's important to be aware of self-deception. Making excuses about someone's behavior and hoping he or she will change signals that you are not living in current time. You need to bring yourself into reality and ask yourself, "What's true right now about this person?" Could you accept this person without an agenda for him or her to change?

If you find yourself rationalizing about a relationship, stop and explore your underlying feelings. Here are some common rationalizations people use to avoid honesty in a relationship. Remember, truth is the starting point for affection, connection, and love.

She has a cold exterior but I know deep down she has the potential for loving.

I feel sorry for her, she really needs my help.

He's had a hard life.

I'll be taken care of if we're together.

She has so much potential.

We're soul mates.

You can't just walk away from people.

The sex was so magical.

I'm not perfect either.

I don't know what I'd do alone. It's not so bad. He doesn't hit me.

To stay in reality, ask yourself, "What's true today?" Notice mushy sentimental feelings of wanting to be the rescuing angel. This is not a good basis for a relationship, and rescuers usually find themselves being left eventually. No one wants to feel indebted to another forever. Avoid deluding yourself by thinking that if you are kind enough, sweet enough, good enough, or smart enough you can change another person. Such a plan starts you out on uneven footing, with you in the superior position. So often people will ask, "What can I do to get through to him? How can I get him to understand?" In Buddhism we turn the questions on ourselves and ask, "What am I really feeling? Why do I expect someone who is usually shut down emotionally suddenly to be expressive? Am I avoiding the grief I will feel if I leave?"

Relationships can't be "fixed" unilaterally. It takes two people willing to become open and seen by the other. It's like creating a dance in which you both lead and follow. You cherish each other's foibles, you laugh at the stories you concoct, and see the humanness in each other.

It may take some internal rewiring to break the old patterns of going to people who are unavailable or harmful. You may have to walk away from your initial impulses and call on your rational mind to assist you. Remember that when you combine head and heart you come closer to wisdom.

Melinda told this story: "I went through a period of being attracted to charming, bright, emotionally withholding men who'd appear to care and then disappear. I think most of them had an alcohol or marijuana problem or were unable to commit. Initially, their charm and friendliness tapped a longing to feel loved that was incredibly powerful. It was like falling under a spell in which I lost hold of reality. I'd feel miserable waiting for them to call or worrying if they really cared. When we were together it was sometimes wonderful and other times they were distant. I usually had a knot in the pit of my stomach.

"After suffering through three such relationships I said to myself, 'Okay, that's it! I don't care if I feel dazzled, turned on, charmed, and my hormones are going wild with attraction. If I see such a person, I'll turn and walk away.' It was very difficult, like pulling back from a force field that had a huge pull. But as I kept doing it I felt relieved, as if there was an adult in charge, protecting me. Eventually (a couple years later), I could stand back and see the seduction game and I didn't even feel tempted to go there. This was also a lonely period because I wasn't attracted to the nice guys who liked me and wanted to be with me—they weren't exciting enough.

"Finally, in looking deeper into myself I saw how much of a little girl I was by wanting someone to charm me, take care of me, and protect me. Eventually I met a man who clearly wanted to be with me. He was reliable and fun, and I didn't have chronic knots in my stomach. The hardest part was to see him as a fallible human being—a peer, an equal. I didn't get to be a little girl with the perfect man . . . well, daddy. A true connection developed and it became a warm-hearted, treasured relationship."

It's helpful to understand the differences between impulse, attraction, and a balanced response to someone. If you've had difficulty forming reciprocal relationships, remember that impulse or strong attraction is often *one* part of yourself reacting to a person. While happy, enduring relationships usually have a strong component of physical attraction, if you're someone with a history of troubled relationships, you'll probably make far better choices when you combine heart, body, hormones, interest, *and* your rational mind. It's like the committee of who you are making the decision, not just one part taking over. For example, a person may be a good fit in terms of interests, but there is no sexual attraction. That's fine if you're friends, but a sad story when it becomes a long-term sexless marriage. Conversely, there may be raging hormones but little else to hold you together.

As you are creating a circle of friends and lovers, reach out, join in the dance, bring your wisest self into the conversation, be willing to reflect on yourself, and go toward that which helps you find out what a precious jewel you are.

To quote the Sufi poet Hafiz,

> *We have not come here to take prisoners,*
> *but to surrender ever more deeply to freedom and joy . . .*
> *Run my dear,*
> *from anything*
> *that may not strengthen*
> *Your precious budding wings . . .*
>
> *For we have not come here to take prisoners*
> *Or to confine our wondrous spirits*
> *But to experience ever and ever more deeply*
> *Our divine courage, freedom, and Light!*

37. Why Do I Freeze Up and Go Silent? Move Beyond the Separating Power of Shame

Shame is a great paralyzer. To become unstuck we need to explore this troublesome feeling. When people are left, excluded, shunned, or abused, they often slide into persistent shame, which can result in depression, isolation, anxiety, and illness.

Shame is a mired down, wretched feeling that arises in response to believing we are intrinsically bad, worthless, and defective. It can become a visceral, hardwired reaction that stems from having been humiliated, degraded, embarrassed, and diminished into an object for someone else's use. Shame is like an old experience ready to be resurrected when someone talks or responds to you in a way that echoes an earlier shaming situation. For example, if someone in the past frequently implied or referred to you as stupid, feelings of shame can be instantly triggered in current time when anyone so much as implies you've done something wrong. When this happens, you are basically reliving an experience from the past and falling into a child state. The reaction is often a wish to disappear, hide, punish yourself, retaliate, defend, or give up on yourself. When this happens, we tend to avert our eyes, blush, collapse in the chest, close the heart, isolate, and sometimes slink away as if in disgrace. The flow within the body becomes constricted.

In *Power vs. Force*, David R. Hawkins calibrates the vibrational level of various emotions or levels of human consciousness, ranging from zero (dead) to 1,000 (enlightenment). He puts Gandhi at 700, the highest possible vibration for normal human consciousness. Shame, the lowest vibration, ranks at the very bottom at 20—the closest experience to being dead. With guilt, at 30, there is at least some sense that you are guilty for what you did. Hawkins goes up the vibrational scale through apathy, grief, fear, desire, anger, and pride, which have increasingly higher vibrations of energy but which he considers destructive levels of force that harm individuals, the environment, and society. Above 200, he lists qualities such as courage, neutrality, willingness, acceptance, reason, love, joy, peace, and enlightenment. I would add gratitude, compassion, and understanding to the list. Because we vary in different situations, no person is a fixed number, but we usually have a range that typifies how we live.

Shame keeps us from learning. If you're taking music lessons, for example, and you translate every suggestion the teacher makes into, "I'm no good, I have no talent, I'll never make it," you are creating a lot of inner anxiety, which blocks learning. Shame is like a non-stop negative evaluator that thwarts fascination and curiosity because you're so worried about being judged as bad or wrong. And, unfortunately, trying to prove you are smart, talented, good, and right won't counteract it; it will just lead to inner combat.

Shame also keeps us stuck because it stops us from taking action—you don't apply for a new job, tell your partner you're upset, take a class, try a new venture, or value your talents because you're afraid of feeling shame if you're turned down (which you call rejected), you make a mistake (you're not perfect), or if someone doesn't want to spend time with you (they're abandoning you).

To counter entrenched feelings of shame, some people blame, counterattack, change the subject, get defensive, make excuses, become arrogant or cruel, or exert power over others through leadership roles. They appear in charge but do great harm with little apparent understanding of their impact on others. Addictions often are a cover for a feeling of deep shame.

Ultimately, shame blocks our wisdom, care, love, creativity, and ability to relax and feel at ease.

Because shame is such a distasteful feeling, people avoid it like the plague. Here are a few people recalling their feelings of shame:

"When I was a kid I used to wish the earth would crack open and swallow me up, I felt so bad. It's not that I wanted to die so much as I wanted to disappear."

"I understand now that my demanding and screaming and yelling was all about covering up my shame. I felt so rotten about myself I'd make a lot of noise to drown out the feelings."

"When my wife would say she was going to spend time with her friends, I'd get terribly jealous and try to stop her. Underneath it was shame, as if I wasn't enough, I'd done something wrong, I wasn't lovable."

"My perfectionism is about shame. I'm not lovable unless I please everyone and always have the right answer. It's as if I've got to perform to get love or friendship because I'm so intrinsically unlovable. The worst part is that I hate myself when I make mistakes, or am not chosen first."

People often feel shame as a result of poverty, racism, homophobia, or sexism. As a community we alleviate shame by providing access to health care, education, decent housing, and community support. Feeling included in a safety net that treats people with respect and encouragement helps counteract feelings of exclusion and being somehow inferior, often a source of shame. We are not isolated individuals so much as communities of people in which the well-being of one affects the well-being of all.

EXERCISE:
Easing Your Feelings of Shame

1. *Name it. Observe it.* When you feel shame, say to yourself some version of the following: "There's the *feeling* of shame. What happened or what did I say to myself before feeling it?" (That I'm bad, I'm unlovable because I made a mistake, hurt someone's feelings, or was left out of the party?)

2. *Realize you are not your shame.* Say to yourself, "This shame is not my essential self. It is an intruder, like toxic chemicals, pollution. It was put there when I was abused, left, hurt, shamed, seduced, teased, neglected, scolded, or not allowed to voice my thoughts or feelings."

3. *Think of what you don't do for yourself because of your shame, and then give yourself the assignment of doing it anyhow.* This could include standing up for yourself, expressing feelings, initiating a conversation, asking for what you need, inviting someone to get together with you.

Having a feeling of mastery over yourself in current time helps counteract the old experience.

4. *Imagine having a new response to a shameful situation.* Imagine being centered, confident, and at peace with yourself in a situation that has previously triggered shame. For example, you could say to someone, "It's not all right to talk to me like that," or "Please ask me what you want without all the innuendos about how I did it wrong." You could also try, "Something about this conversation doesn't feel right, and I need to end it for now," or "Could you tell me what you meant by that?" or even, "That feels like a shaming remark—was that your intention?"

5. *Don't defend against other people's shaming remarks or comments about yourself.* For example, if someone says (or implies) you are wearing a weird shirt, agree with them, "Yeah, it's funky, I like it." If someone says, "This cake isn't as good as last time you made it," reply, "I agree (if you do); it did turn out better before," or "Really? It seems the same to me."

6. *If you get triggered into shame, call someone who is understanding and has a sense of humor.* Keep a list by the phone because in a shame state you will probably forget that you have any friends. You might even set something up in advance. "Could I call you for support when I'm upset or feeling bad?"

7. *Read Stephen Wolinsky's book Quantum Consciousness,* which has numerous exercises you can use to deal with shame.

8. *Go into big mind.* "I am feeling *the* shame of being used or hurt. I am feeling *the* shame of exploiting others or hurting them. I am having *the* human experience of feeling shame. I am not alone. There are many people feeling shame right this moment. It's just a feeling, it will all pass."

38. Connect by Listening: Set Your Opinions Aside, at Least for a While

> What I want in my life is compassion,
> a flow between myself and others
> based on mutual giving from the heart.
> —MARSHALL B. ROSENBERG,
> NONVIOLENT COMMUNICATION

Understanding is at the heart of Buddhism. *In many ways it is the core of love.* To be seen, known, and accepted is to feel loved. Understanding and attuning to others is a deep form of meditation, as it allows us to become a witness to another person's world as our mind becomes quiet and our body relaxed and receptive. It's about attunement rather than judgment, resonance rather than separation.

People who don't listen well, who interrupt, get restless inside, want to smooth over difficulties, take the conversation back to themselves, are usually uneasy with feelings, or their ego self has its own need to be heard and validated. Thus, the ability to listen attentively is truly a measure of our inner peace.

Deep listening is a blessing and a gift to others. To listen is to let go of the self and be fully present for another person—even when they have strong feelings. When our intent is to resonate truly with what our friend is experiencing, we become bonded in the "us" place. This relates to getting unstuck because when we feel connected and seen, every system in our body calms down and feelings of alienation and separation abate. When we have resources for feeling heard, seen, and cared for, we gain the courage and curiosity to crack through our boundaries and expand our lives.

In repeatedly observing people who are "good or relaxed listeners," I've noticed they say very little, while listening with a receptivity, warmth, and steady gaze. They don't take the conversation over to themselves or take sides and rarely interrupt or give advice or attempt to "make" the other person feel better. There is a high level of attunement—the person can feel when it's okay to ask a more personal question or make a suggestion. That's why a guidebook is only part of what's needed; listening is ultimately a reflection of our inner stillness and ability to attune.

If you have trouble listening, you may be uncomfortable with feelings, have lots of judgments and strong opinions, or take the moral high ground, all of which will keep you feeling separate. You may feel anxious when someone disagrees with you or is in emotional turmoil. Notice any quick impulse to give advice, help someone out, or say, "It will be all right," for this is usually done to quell *your* discomfort with uncertainty or pain. At this point, you're not listening; you're reacting out of your own uneasiness or need for attention.

Responding is different than reacting. A response comes from taking in what another person has said, letting it flow through you and listening for what arises within you, then relaying it back to the other person. Sometimes we primarily listen; other times we have a dialogue. True dialogue is an interactive dynamic experience, not just a reiteration of our beliefs—it feels new because we are responding to what arises in the moment while listening deeply within ourselves.

If you are tightly identified with your beliefs, it's hard to listen and be supportive of another person. For example, Ruth, who loved her job, had planned to stay home with her new baby for six weeks before going back to work. Her friend Jill had a strong belief that mothers should stay home with their infants for at least six months. Jill felt upset with Ruth, she worried about the baby, and she found it difficult to be around Ruth. To Jill, it was not a difference of opinion—she believed that she was right and Ruth was wrong and she wanted to convince Ruth to change her plans. At this point Jill could no longer be a responsive friend because she had an agenda for Ruth.

There is a way out of this common dilemma—Jill can have her belief but let go trying to convince Ruth. In other words, the relationship stays in the forefront and her opinions recede to the background. Jill may continue to hold to her belief that it is better for mothers to stay home with children for six months, but she's not righteous about her beliefs; she just has them and can set them aside when Ruth talks about her plans for child care. From this more relaxed state, she can even voice her opinion—once—but it won't come across as judgmental.

If you decide to relate feelings of concern, own them as your need to be honest, so you don't create distance. For example, Jill might say, "I need to tell you this because it's getting in my way of feeling close to you. I really wish you'd find a way to stay home with your new baby longer because I have a strong belief that it's better for the child. I'm saying this because I don't want my belief to come out sideways or get in the way of our friendship. I also want to say that I wish you all the best and want to be of help no matter what you decide."

Another way of staying connected is to avoid a simple right-wrong stance, which Jill did in the first example. Look at the whole picture: Jill can be receptive as Ruth talks about the kind of child care she has found, how much time her husband will be with the baby, the importance of her career, and even her own conflicted feelings about the situation. Jill can remember that there are many variables about good parenting.

By broadening the conversation, seeing it more as a mosaic of many colors, not just a black and white, right and wrong picture, Jill and Ruth stay in the "us" place, which is by nature an unstuck place. They can have their differences *and* stay friends.

If you can change one thing—cease to give advice or stop interrupting—you can dramatically change your relationships as well as your inner experience and the structure of your personality.

EXERCISE:

Notice Your Conversational Habits

1. Pick one aspect of listening or relating you would like to work on and keep a journal on a daily basis. When recalling a situation note how your body felt at the time. For example, most people become aware of revving up inside as they are about to assure the other person, give advice, state an opinion, or talk about their similar experience. Also notice how you feel with silence in a conversation.

    Here are some specific qualities that usually block connection. You might choose one or more of the following or create your own.

    - Notice when you take someone away from strong feelings by getting analytical or making up reasons for another person, such as, "What day did that happen?" "Maybe it's because . . ."
    - Notice when you want to assure someone he or she is okay. "It's okay"; "You shouldn't worry"; "It happens to lots of people."
    - Notice when you interrupt.
    - Notice when you take the conversation back to yourself.
    - Notice when you break eye contact for more than a brief time, or look away and feel restless.
    - Notice when you give advice.
    - Notice when you want to defend or talk someone out of their opinion.
    - Notice when you talk at length, going from one idea to another, and have difficulty coming to a stop. Be especially aware of your body sensations, holding your breath, and the reactions of other people around you. Some people end a sentence with "and" . . . as if waiting for a new idea to arise. Practice saying one or two sentences and stopping.
    - Notice when you relax, feel calm inside, and listen without feeling a need to make a quick response.

- Notice when a conversation feels flowing—easy, relaxed, and natural.

39. Reach Out to Others and Feel the Space in Your Heart

We learned that service is the rent we pay for living. It is the very purpose of life and not something you do in your spare time.
—MARIAN WRIGHT EDELMAN

Healing ourselves and getting unstuck comes from creating a flow within us and between us. The Buddha taught that we are created of one and the same energy, so to become part of the flow of giving and receiving is to move into a circle of connection with all people and become a single cell in the larger body of life.

"How can I be of help?" is a deep question that taps into our strengths and allows us to share our gifts. "What do I have to give?" "What would I enjoy giving?" "What would ease someone else's isolation or suffering?" Parents may express this with their children, it may be offered by smiling at the person at the checkout counter, by teaching English to children from another country, volunteering, helping at a shelter, getting on a board, raising money for a community organization, or walking dogs at the Humane Society.

An excitement and glow often reflect the pleasure of doing for others. For example, I've spoken with numerous women involved in Missoula's first Habitat for Humanity house built completely by women. The project became a place where women could show up, learn new skills, and revel in working together. When the house was completed they held a festive, exciting, and emotional opening celebration. A group of people gathered on the tiny front lawn as a young mother and her two children stood on the porch and were handed the keys to their new home, along with a Bible. Although it was a modest house situated on a back alley, it could have been a palace to see the joy and excitement of this wonderous accomplishment created by many people with loving kindness.

As giving and receiving merge into a single flow, we realize that we are not "the other"; we are part of the whole. We take our gifts and pass them around. And receive the gifts from others.

To allow ourselves to be cared for, helped, encouraged, and taught can be a blessing for others. Just as the giver needs to give because it brings her into a fuller existence, it is a mark of our humanity to receive from others. One of our final tasks in living is to help those we'll leave behind when we die.

Let me tell you about the death of my Grandma Charlotte Davis. Grandma Davis loved me. Of that I was sure. We were kindred spirits—independent, curious, questioning. Our times together in the ten years she lived with our family centered around reading, talking, questioning things, and going to libraries and museums. Whether we were sitting on a park bench, waiting for a bus, resting in a museum, or snuggled up on the couch, there was always a book nearby—in her purse, on the table, or by the bed.

When I was fourteen and she was dying from cancer, every day after school I'd run upstairs to her room to see how she was. For some time she had spent her afternoons resting on the chaise longue. But then one day she said, "I want to go to bed and never get up." I was losing the one person who gave me the gift of her full attention and love. I was devastated to watch her slipping away.

Grandma Davis helped me with my desolation and sorrow through a simple gift I will never forget. One day when I came to her room, she asked me to read some of her favorite poems to her. It had never occurred to me that I would ever be asked to read to the woman who had instilled in me a profound love of learning. In my grief, this act connected me to her in a way that spoke to every moment we had spent together—words, beauty, meaning. Through my tears I could give something back to my grandmother, my namesake who had read to me thousands of times. I don't know if I've ever felt so completely loved and connected to anyone before or since.

I don't believe it is more blessed to give than to receive, the usual words intoned before the donation plate is passed in church. *I believe there is no separation when the giving and receiving are embedded in relationship.* It forms a sacred union between both people. For some people receiving is far more difficult because it challenges the belief that one is undeserving. Receiving can pierce the heart and humble us. I remember my mother, after attending an Alzheimer's support group when my father was dying, saying in a heartfelt way, "People really do care, don't they?" It appeared to be a surprise to her.

Being of help raises many spiritual questions because it can easily lead to sentiment, condescension, or ego gratification. "See, I'm being a good person." *At the purest level, giving doesn't exist, because we don't truly own anything.* All things are One Energy. We are simply channels for whatever has been given to us. As recipients and givers our paths converge, each of us sharing our unique selves and gifts.

Steven Harrison, in *Doing Nothing*, writes, "Giving without relationship creates an object out of a human being. Our responsibility to help is the responsibility to relate. In relationship, we discover that the divisions that thought creates dissolve into wholeness."

Move from Thought to Action

Whatever you can do, or dream you can, begin it.
Boldness has genius, magic and power in it. Begin it now.
—GOETHE, MOBILIZING THE FORCES OF THE UNIVERSE

40. Find Your Fire, the Source of Transformation

> It is not enough to be compassionate. You must act. There are two aspects to action. One is to overcome the distortions and afflictions of your own mind ... The other is more social, more public. When something needs to be done in the world to rectify the wrongs, if one is really concerned with benefitting others, one needs to be engaged, involved.
>
> —THE DALAI LAMA, THE PATH TO TRANQUILITY

Ultimately in life, you take action or you don't. All the talk, analyzing, insight, and dreams are only interesting ideas until you put them into action. The challenge is to find your fire, the energy of transformation, and use it to mobilize your intentions in a sustained, organized direction. Fire creates the alchemy that mixes together your hopes, desires, and dreams and converts them into, "I can, I will, and here's my plan."

Siddhartha Gautama reached a state of enlightenment through the actions he took. It started with an inner restlessness and curiosity about the causes of suffering, which eventually turned into his life's path. This overarching desire led him to slip past the protective eyes of his father and walk around the city to explore the world beyond his sheltered existence. He experimented with the spiritual practices of his time but eventually abandoned them because they were not helping him to actualize his goal of understanding the cause of suffering.

Taking action was cyclical for Siddhartha Gautama, just as it is in most of our lives. He'd try an approach, learn from it, see if it led to his vision, reevaluate, and then try something else. In other words, the cycle requires you to listen for your truths, follow them with appropriate action, then ask yourself, "Does this work? Does this action take me where I want to go? Is it creating greater joy and peace of mind and helping me find out who I am?" If not, you need to be willing to make a change.

Taking action in a Buddhist context is not about attaining something out there—having status, possessions, money—it's about living now, being guided by the essence of who you are. It's about clearing out whatever keeps you preoccupied, rigid, self-absorbed, worried, suffering.

The fuel for your fire is a burning desire to live your own life—to reach for the deepest parts of yourself, to give birth to who you are, to know happiness, peace of mind, and freedom. It is built upon a deeply felt refusal to be stuck, bored, depressed, and unhappy for long periods of time. Fire is the energizer that becomes a commitment to do whatever it takes to actualize your intentions: leave, move, propose, take a break, get a new job, finish tasks, clear the air, invite people over, practice yoga, get more sleep, paint the kitchen, or go where you feel a pull.

Once a commitment is made, a whole stream of events may present themselves to carry us on our way. W. H. Murray, speaking of his Himalayan expedition, put it this way:

> The moment one definitely commits oneself, providence moves too.
> All sorts of things occur to help one that would have not otherwise
> have occurred.
>
> —W. H. Murray, *The Scottish Himalayan Expedition,*
> 1950

Some people might consider it magical thinking to believe that providence moves with us, but the evidence of this experience is compelling. Whether providence moves, or we become open, observant, receptive, and willing to utilize anything that comes our way, commitment does sets energy in motion. Taking action in a Buddhist context bridges the inner duality of believing one way and living another. I asked a woman who had left a relationship and moved back to the area, "What prompted you to leave?" "I was tired of being a sad story," she replied, leaving nothing else to say.

Sometimes we take action to get out of a dreary or unfulfilling situation. The person who once loved teaching school quits to be free from daily classroom preparation. The manager of a store decides that sixty-hour weeks and working weekends is ruining her family life, and steps down. A young woman who worked in a local diner for three years walks out and says, "Okay, I'm willing to go back to school to get my GED and some vocational training. I don't want to sweat the rest of my life away in a greasy kitchen."

From a Buddhist perspective, it's not just about taking action, it's about taking "right" action by considering the far-reaching implications of your actions on yourself, your loved ones, and your environment. This does not preclude buying a house or owning something, but you don't do these things as an attempt to change your image. You remain who you are and happen to live in a nice house. The direction we are going is toward ease, non-duality, non-grasping, and acceptance of whatever is happening inside you. So, as you consider taking action, remember you are going toward your true self.

What are the actions you want to take in your life? How many times have you said, "I need to exercise more, eat better, save money, call that old friend, get rid of the junk, or improve my work situation"? The following chapters will help you to mobilize your energy to sustain whatever it takes to help you live more fully in the center of your life.

41. Re-Circuit Your Brain by Taking Action

A thing rests by changing.
—HERACLITUS

People who are masters at getting unstuck bring a lively mind to everyday situations. When things go wrong there may be a moment of upset, but then the mind switches gears and asks, "Okay, what can I do about it?" It doesn't become a drama or a bad luck story to repeatedly tell. It's more like, "Here's life right now, what am I going to do to be one with it? What actions, large or small, do I need to take to keep the flow in my body, mind, and spirit?" This doesn't mean you fix everything the minute it's broken; it means you are highly attuned to your inner world and when you find congestion, either in relationships or your lifestyle, you notice it and move toward action so you don't get stuck around it. It often takes less energy to move forward than to resist change.

Unstuck thinking includes being playful, creative, willing to experiment, make changes, and bring a freshness to every day. It's about looking outside the box for answers to little questions, being alive to all of one's senses: seeing, hearing, attuning, questioning, and noticing what brings joy, variety, and beauty to our lives. It often includes breaking with traditional sex roles.

For example, a dear friend, Tory, who was feeling mired down with her responsibility for keeping a home for her husband and three adolescent boys, announced one day that she was retiring from food service forever. After a family discussion, they got out a calendar and everyone signed up for a night of cooking and cleaning up, rotating through the five of them on a continuing basis. They also gave up having fixed places to sit at the dinner table. As Tory said to me, "I was complaining about *having to cook*, then I thought, who says I have to do this! These kids can learn how to cook and so can Arnie."

This change dramatically shifted the constellation of the family in terms of power, entitlement, responsibility, and sex roles. In a few years the boys all became excellent cooks and Tory never felt resentful or trapped in a role that didn't work for her.

This sounds like a small thing, but is it, actually? Small changes often lie at the vortex of huge changes in one's outlook and sense of mastery. Think of how Tory's boys gained a new perspective on women and family responsibilities. They went from a sense of entitlement to contributing to the basic meal routines. Imagine how their mother's self-respecting act would be carried into her sons' marriages and passed on to the next generation. Imagine how her willingness to cast tradition aside helped them to question all habitual rituals and rules.

In talking with Tory's husband, Arnie, he said with a laugh, "The kids were really surprised to see that I'd cook too and that we'd all pitch in. It was completely different from how I was raised and what I initially expected in a family . . . but it was great, it brought us all closer together and Tory is much happier. So are we."

By breaking one fixed ritual, you open the door to be able to reexamine everything. You create flexibility in the mind—kind of like re-circuiting old neurological habits.

In an interview on National Public Radio, Dr. Joseph LeDoux, a neuroscientist at New York University, and Dr. Jack Forman, a research psychiatrist at Columbia University, talked about the ability to take action and its effect on the brain and our emotional states. When Dr. LeDoux saw on videotape the pipe bomb explosion at the 1996 Summer Olympics in Atlanta, he noticed how the crowd froze until one person started running, and then everyone started running. He wondered exactly what happened in the brain in that moment between freezing and taking action. Dr. LeDoux's research revealed a fear circuit in the amygdala of the brain that commands people to freeze in response to danger or trauma. If we stay in this frozen state, however, we fall into passive helplessness, which can lead to despondency and depression. Over time we may become avoidant and withdrawn and feel like a victim.

On the other hand, according to LeDoux, the signal that commands freeze can be rerouted to a part of the amygdala that commands, "Move to action." This happens when you repeatedly take deliberate actions in the face of trauma and fear. As LeDoux says, "Even if you feel paralyzed with fear, make that move." It's like throwing a switch in the circuitry of the amygdala that relays messages to the parts of the brain to help it mobilize for action. Over time, as you respond to difficulties with active problem solving, you retrain the brain to automatically throw the switch to the part that says, "Take action."

According to LeDoux, when the brain circuit switches from freeze to take action, it's the brain's way of moving on and letting go of trauma so you can get on with your life. If you are afraid of speaking up for yourself, you do it anyhow. If you are in a painful situation, you take action to change it or walk away. If you are uneasy about doing something good for yourself, you go ahead and do it. If you are grieving the loss of a loved one, you can have your sadness, *and* also take action to bring pleasure, connection, and joy back into your life. The brain will respond accordingly and help you get past the feelings of helplessness or despondency.

The science of switching the brain circuitry is analogous to fire as the energy that moves us to action. Fire moves upward, destroying, transforming, heating up our lives. Taking action in the present helps us step beyond the past, as we move beyond old conditioning of fear and helplessness and affirm our right to live, enjoy, and have the life we want. Even if there is a history of trauma, taking action can have a dramatic effect, contributing to a sense of mastery and power over your life.

EXERCISE:

Take Action

1. Make a list of actions you can take to help your life be more enjoyable.

2. Make a list of actions that will counteract the habitual responses that keep you stuck. Give yourself assignments—take one action at a time and follow through with it, discomfort, fear, and all.

42. Ground Yourself to Ease Your Fears

We can use the martial arts approach to grounding when we approach change that feels challenging or scary. Grounding is about feeling yourself solidly rooted on the ground, strong *and* relaxed, alert *and* quiet, flexible *and* centered. If you stay grounded as you head into the unknown, making change will not seem so daunting, whether it's facing inner pain or taking on a challenging task.

I observed a remarkable example of grounding in a workshop: two people paired up; one was instructed to stand straight up and put their arm out and the other was to try to get them off center by pressing down on their arm, which they did easily. On a second try, the standing people were taught to flex their knees, drop their pelvis, imagine flexible roots from their feet going down into the ground, make some deep belly sounds—Ho!—then imagine their torso as powerful and strong, yet flexible, and their arms as extensions of the torso. Keeping that image, they were instructed to sway gently while staying grounded. When the partners again tried to pull them off center by pressing down on their arm, they were unable to do so.

You can also ground yourself with thoughts, especially if you draw them deeply into yourself, like energy into your whole body. *For example, when you're approaching a task or relationship:*

- I'd like this to go a certain way, but if it doesn't I'll still be all right.
- Whatever happens means nothing about my "worth."
- I can always ask for help if I get stuck.
- People say yes and people say no; you win some you lose some—that's life.
- Whatever happens is not headline news—it's just a little moment in the great expanse of time.
- I can choose to quit if something doesn't feel right.

People often feel ungrounded as a result of the way they handle emotions: they either restrict their thoughts and feelings, which makes their bodies rigid and unyielding, or tend to be awash in an ever-changing sea of emotions, which keeps them overwhelmed. Grounding can help us feel safe to have our feelings without getting overwhelmed.

EXERCISE

Ground Yourself to Take Action

If you're with another person, one can read this to the other.

- Sit (or stand) with your feet solidly on the floor or rug. Breathe, relax your belly, drop your shoulders, and say to yourself, "Let go."
- Bring your focus to your solar plexus or belly and imagine a centered place, a source of strength. Take all the time you need.

- Imagine this place as a source of energy. Feel the energy expand throughout your body, becoming brighter, stronger, going into your muscles, bones, blood, heart, and mind. Take time with this. It should feel fluid, and perhaps full or heavy.

- Then imagine this energy dropping down through your belly, pelvis, legs, and right into the ground. Be aware of your feet connecting with the floor. Again, take all the time you need. Some people use images such as light energy moving through their body and down into the ground; others see roots going down through their legs and into the earth; still others have a sense of weight moving downward through their body or an increased feeling of gravity.

- Now undulate, sway, and move your upper body with a sense of energy going upward. Be sure to relax your shoulders and soften your body. Notice the sensations in your body.

- Now imagine an action you want to take, including all the steps—gathering resources, asking for help, making phone calls, thinking about what to say. Start at the very beginning or preparatory stages. Take time with each step. Close your eyes, experience yourself going through the steps as if they are actually happening, while staying grounded. You might feel as if your feet start to "disappear," or you hear saboteurs discouraging you. If this happens, go back to grounding yourself.

- If you get anxious or uneasy, come back and focus on your grounding.

- Repeat the above steps, imagining yourself taking action until you can walk through the whole process. With practice you will train your nervous system to feel grounded, thus able to take action when a difficult situation arises or you are afraid and uneasy.

43. Manage Your Energy, Not Just Your Time

Anything that crowds the life out of you is junk.
—DON ASLETT

People often talk about managing time, but what we're really managing is our energy. Think of yourself as a vortex of motion with a continuing cycle of energy moving through you. Managing energy goes beyond the concept of energy coming in and going out—it's keeping the energy alive within you no matter what you are doing. Notice the situations and people that spark your interest, emotions, and excitement, and those that lead to feeling heavy, dull, or drained.

Efficiency is about getting the most done with the least output of energy. This applies to sports, organizing your home, taking on projects, playing a musical instrument, or running a business. In response to my request at a recent tennis lesson to "hit harder," the teacher had me work at relaxing deeper, getting in the correct position, and expending more energy only when speeding up the racket at the point of contact with the ball. It was amazing—much less energy output, and a much faster shot.

A first step to becoming more efficient with your energy on the home front is to cut out extraneous tasks and get yourself organized so you're not always running out of dog food, frustrated looking for important papers, or scurrying around in the morning looking for socks that match. Notice what you often misplace and create a place for it. Then stop, focus on the place, and, for example, say to yourself, "I will always put my car keys here when I walk in the house." Do this until it becomes a habit.

I had an office assistant named Linda who, in her first interview said, "I can do in twelve hours what it takes other people twenty hours to do." And she was right. Within a day, the jumble of pens and pencils on the desk was reduced to four—red, black, and blue pens and a pencil. When I commented on it she said, "Why would I want to waste my life shuffling around in a bunch of pens when this is all I need?" Everything was within easy reach and all extraneous items had been deposited in a box. She had suggestions for a new filing system and told me about a used office supply place where we could get a good buy on some low files.

When we started going through a stack of things on the desk she'd ask, "Where does it go?" and she'd get up and put it there, even if it meant going to another part of the house. Her theme song was, "Do it now, now, now!" Doing things now is also a theme in Buddhism. Be here now—eyes, ears, mind, breath, body—be present right now, be with whatever is going on. Don't save life for later.

Because Linda could work faster and more efficiently, I paid her more per hour, so she could go home earlier and take a five mile walk with a friend. And that's the point of being efficient. *Efficiency is not some moral virtue; rather, it gives you time to do the things that bring you pleasure and time to relax.*

Managing your energy often includes giving up perfectionism. Perfectionism creates tension and stress as we focus on getting everything done just right—often by someone else's standards—as opposed to completing the task sufficiently and staying relaxed. If there's a recurring theme I hear in my therapy practice it's people feeling discouraged by an internal critic saying, "You never do anything good enough." We need to pick and choose what needs meticulous attention and what doesn't need to be so perfect.

Jack, whom I counseled with his wife, Kristin, complained bitterly of never having enough time to relax and have fun. When he complained about taking care of the yard, the house, the dog, and so on, Kristin broke in and said, "But Jack, you take three hours to mow the yard perfectly when I can do an okay job in forty-five minutes. It doesn't need to be so perfect—the grass will grow back anyhow." Think through the tasks that can be done less perfectly if you feel stressed for time. In other words, there's nothing wrong with taking three hours to mow the yard if you have the time and enjoy it, but if you're feeling stressed, do a reasonable job and save time for fun. There is a scene in *Robinson Crusoe* when Crusoe and Friday are building a canoe together and Crusoe tells his cohort, Friday, that it's time to declare the task is done. In other words, it's good enough, let's go to the next step.

Take time to get organized. It's calming to know you can reach for something and find it in a predictable place. It basically takes a file drawer (or a box) and some file folders with labels like "unpaid bills," "tax information," "birth certificate." It's also helpful to have a calendar to write down notes such as "insurance payment due." Not having a system to pay bills on time costs us in late fees, a feeling of chaos, and a bad credit rating. It can mean driving to town in heavy traffic to make a car payment at the last possible moment instead of mailing it two days earlier. Compare the energy cost of getting frantic, using an hour of time, and feeling frustrated, plus the cost of gas, with putting a 37 cent stamp on an envelope and dropping it in your mailbox. This might sound like one small thing, but multiply it by ten little stresses a week and you join the ranks of people who chronically say, "Sorry I didn't get back to you, my life has been crazy lately."

If you tend to be chaotic or inefficient, take some time to create a system. Schedule time on your calendar to actualize your plan, as in: "Tuesday evening I'm going to buy file folders, three-ring binders, paper and dividers, markers, and a desk calendar. Wednesday, during my lunch hour, I'm going to the hardware store for duct tape, screws to fix things, and a duplicate key to hide so I don't get locked out again." Many people know what needs to be done but don't get to it, even if it would mean saving a lot of time and hassle. If you can't get started, ask a friend to help you, or hire someone, or go to FlyLady.net, a totally encouraging, non-shaming help line for getting organized.

Managing energy isn't about always having everything done; it's about balancing the important things in life. I remember a balmy summer night in Athens, Ohio, rocking on my front porch swing; there was a ten-foot expanse between my porch and Millie Bean's porch, and Millie would be there swaying in her rocking chair, fanning herself, and occasionally spraying mosquitos. My daughter referred to Millie Bean as her grandma-next-door, because she could always go there for company or a long sit on her ample lap.

When I commented, "I should go in and clean up," Millie said, "Aw, stay and talk to me. The dirt will still be there." And she was right—the dirt stayed but she wasn't there much longer, and I'm glad I kept swinging away and talking with her on that hot muggy night. The point is to choose between letting some things go, doing what is essential, and then taking time to relax. Grass and dust will wait; the time to enjoy your loved ones is now. What lasts in our hearts are the memories of feeling close to those we love.

Being efficient is also about making life restful so you have clear energy for the important things. It is not uncommon for people in the United States to be on the move from morning to night without a break. Contrast this to England, for example, where tea time is an institution in which everything stops. You sit, have tea, and chat, uninterrupted by anything else. This brings to mind the Eastern tradition of bowing and saying namaste—I salute the divinity/light in you—whenever you meet someone. There's a pause, acknowledgment, and a moment of quiet, similar to taking a deep breath.

Take the pause that refreshes. Part of restfulness is about doing one thing at a time interspersed with breaks to rest. This brings to mind going for a music coaching session with the violinist I accompanied many years ago at Professor Blatt's home. The professor, who was of German descent, was the opera conductor at the University. We were cordially greeted and invited to sit down for tea and cookies, all nicely arranged at a table. After our friendly chat, during which Professor Blatt showed complete interest in our lives, we got to work, and I mean work—intense, emotional, and directive as in: "No! No! Softer, softer . . . let it relax. Now, let it flow, there, that's right. Now do it again. Again." The impression I took from that experience was that being totally immersed in whatever you are doing—be it a pause or an activity—brings a great richness to life, and a deep sense of order.

Preserving your energy also means taking care not to get drained by relationships. The first step is to be more direct, forthright, and connected to your emotions in your conversations with family and friends. Take the fewest number of words to be kind and say what's true. You can start your sentences out with phrases such as, "I like it when," "I don't like it when," "I feel happy when," "I feel upset when." Or, for example, you could say, "Here's what I'd like to do, how do you feel about that?" "Thanks a lot for the invitation, but I'm not able to come. I'd love to see you another time."

Clients will sometimes say that they talked about "it" for three hours. The truth doesn't take much time when you are in touch with your emotions and are direct about what you want. People get lost in a jungle of analyzing, making points, explaining, justifying, or making links to childhood, but the real connection comes when you say, "I'm afraid you'll leave." "I love it when you smile at me that way." "I'd like to take a trip to a lake together this weekend." That's real.

This doesn't preclude talking about your day, or telling stories around a camp fire, but even then, the more you talk from the core of your experience and include your emotions, the more engaging it will be.

A second aspect of preserving your energy in relationships can mean taking yourself out of some situations, not taking on other people's problems, and managing difficult relationships you want to maintain. You may need to extricate yourself from a draining conversation by either addressing what is troublesome about the conversation or kindly interrupting and saying, "Excuse me for interrupting, but I need to go now." This is a huge step for some people because it affirms your right to take care of yourself. It doesn't mean you are rude, uncaring, mean, or selfish, although some people will say you are because they perceive limit setting as a withdrawal of friendship.

Some relationships may begin to ebb if you start to take better care of yourself. Just as all life is in motion, it's natural to have a shift in friendships, while maintaining the treasured ones that endure.

You can also learn to manage your energy in difficult relationships you want to maintain because of history or family ties. For example, if visiting a cantankerous parent in a nursing home leaves you feeling undone, create strategies to protect your energy: go less often, go more often for less time, take a friend with you, arrive at three and say you have an appointment at four, bring a story to read or some music to play, or ask her to tell stories about her childhood.

It can also help to talk with other people in similar situations to relieve your guilt. Most of all, stop saying things such as, "I *should* like visiting her, she's my mother." Guilt is very dense energy. The truth is you don't like visiting her, and that's reality. It doesn't make you a bad person; it's just "what is." To soften your heart you can send prayers, cards, light energy, and good wishes but remember to send them to yourself as well.

We manage our energy so we can enjoy life and feel the aliveness that we are. We de-junk our lives, be it things, relationships, rituals, or habits, so we can be free.

> *That which restricts our living, loving, thinking, and feeling is junk, be it a thing, habit, person, place or position. Anything that builds, edifies, enriches our spirit—that makes us truly happy regardless of how worthless it may be in cash terms—isn't junk.*
> —DON ASLETT, *CLUTTER'S LAST STAND*

44. Focus on Everything You Have to Gain by Taking Action

Some people get jump-started into taking action because they hit bottom, to use an addiction expression, and feel terrified. They may be whacked with many painful consequences of their behavior, have several brushes with death, or experience life as so pervasively awful, empty, and exhausting that they finally get motivated to do something hard to make it better. Hopefully many of us will make change before getting to this point.

One way to energize yourself to start something new is to focus on all you have to gain by making changes in your life. It's like looking forward to the exhilaration you'll feel at the end of a run, having a reliable car because you saved enough money to buy it, feeling closer to your loved ones because you took time to talk over difficulties, getting a better job after you finish school, feeling the delight of a cleaned-up home. It's about casting your vision into the big picture of your life instead of hanging on to the small comforts of lying on the couch, watching TV, drinking, or not exerting yourself to look for a better job or get more education. You might ask yourself, "How will I feel if my life is the same in one year? in five? in ten?"

I live in a town full of transplants, many of whom passed through, fell in love with the place, and uprooted themselves to be in this beautiful valley intersected by two rivers and surrounded by mountains full of hiking trails. The prevailing feeling is that people are happy to be here—they feel excited, grateful, and lucky. It creates a sparkling atmosphere that fosters creativity and community involvement.

What are the dreams drifting around in the recesses of your mind? What is your image of the life you'd like? Bring these thoughts to the forefront and imagine how you would feel if you took a step in that direction . . . and then another one.

Do any of the following thoughts resonate with you as you imagine yourself taking the steps necessary for change?

I'd feel happier.

I'd have more energy.

I'd feel more confident.

I wouldn't worry so much.

Life would be more exciting.

I'd have closer relationships.

I'd be more relaxed.

I'd be living what I believe.

I'd be healthier.

I'd be learning something new.

Other, other, other.

As a variation, you can create an image of having already made the change. Picture it in your mind's eye with details of where you are and what you are doing. Breathe into the thoughts and sensations, let them expand throughout your body, make them brighter, stronger, more expansive.

Continue to imagine that the change has already happened. I am sober; I've moved; I take a walk several days a week; I am meditating regularly. If fears, saboteurs, or censors arise, walk them into a waiting room, sit down, and shut the door and come back to the positive visualization. I'll discuss several processes to work with this later on. Finally, persevere. If you get off track, be kind to yourself and start again. Keep your focus on all you have to gain and notice how you feel—physically and emotionally.

45. Explore the Eight Steps That Take You from Thought to Action

Now that you've spent time focusing on what you'd like to change, and all you have to gain, you've set the stage for taking action.

1. Feel the inner swirl of not taking action. When you have needs, goals, or ideas of how you want to live differently but don't take action, you might become a living, swirling whirlpool of energy with no direction or outlet. It's as if your hopes, goals, thoughts, excuses, rationalizations, guilt, irritation at yourself, get put in a mixing bowl and churn around inside your body, creating pressure and going nowhere. You might feel both dull and chaotic with spurts of energy going in random directions. You might be caught in some familiar thoughts:

"The boyfriend is not good for me, but I don't want to give up being part of a couple."

"I want to be sober, but I can't imagine living without alcohol to fall back on when I'm upset."

"I want to live more simply, but I keep taking on too many projects, buying too much stuff, and getting myself in debt."

"I want to be slim, but I can't say no to sweets and that second helping of pasta."

These dualities can range from a nagging little voice that arises periodically to a chronic state of congestion, agitation, or unhappiness. Being out of sync with yourself is revealed in your body and mind: you might experience frustration, pain, repetitive thoughts, low energy, body tension, and compulsions, all swirling around inside, directionless and chaotic.

2. See the big picture. Name the concern and explore everything about it. The first step out of the swirl (also known as overwhelm, a speeding mind, worry, and anxiety) is to slow it down, focus on one concern, and take it apart so you can see it and calm yourself. Don't talk in swirl language by endlessly recounting the trials and tribulations of your life to yourself and others. This will only cause your body to tense up and secrete the stress hormone cortisol. It's much more useful to breathe, drop your shoulders, and soften your belly and relax. Remember, solutions often arise from a state of alert calm as we gain a different perspective.

Take one concern or goal you'd like to explore more deeply. What's stopping you? What are you afraid of? Although the situation may appear to have a simple answer, many times it's part of a bigger picture involving time, money, responsibilities, energy, and inner saboteurs. And remember, on the path of getting unstuck, all roads lead to Rome. In other words, if you can change one thing that has you stuck, you will loosen up the knots of resistance and be more able to change something else.

Look at all aspects of a concern. For example, if the chronic mess in your house upsets you, explore what the problem is really about. Do you need more storage shelves? Coat hooks in the front hall? A plan for everyone in the house? To get rid of stuff? To hire someone to help you? To feel less depressed? To let go of sentiment connected to your excess stuff?

As another example, if you are unhappy or bored in your job, ask, Is it about the work itself? My relationship with my boss? The salary? The work load? Relationships with other employees? A dead end path? Too far to commute?

If you are troubled in a relationship, you might ask, Do I know what's troubling me? Am I afraid to bring it up? Have we talked about it fully? Would counseling help? Do I have too many expectations? Would more time together help? Am I staying because I'm afraid to give up the financial security (which leads to another set of questions to explore)? Is it fully clear that I want to leave and need to make a plan to do so?

Think of one thing you can do to address one piece of the problem or list a possible sequence of actions, and put them on a calendar. Make a date with yourself to do them. Even if it's just a phone call to get information, write it down and say when you will do it. Taking that first step is like turning a key in the stuck place and changing gears.

3. Set your intention. Resolve to change the situation.

> *Setting an intention is about getting really focused. It's so much about owning your stuff and not blaming anyone else. It's like saying, I'm going to take responsibility for my happiness, my life, my everything.*
>
> —DODIE MOQUIN, PSYCHOTHERAPIST

We move closer to taking action when we have a talk with ourselves: okay enough of this. I've said for three years I'm going to stop yelling at the kids/take a parenting class, exercise, eat better, start looking for a new job, take steps to improve our sex life/relationship, and I'm still not doing it. I'm going to figure out what this is about and change it. You feel the fire rising. Very often it helps to call a friend and ask them to either help you or be your cheering squad. Tell them exactly when you plan to take one step, and ask if you can call them for a verbal high five when you follow through.

Setting an intention takes us another step out of the swirl. It needs to be more than a New Year's resolution to change a behavior. It means you are going to expand the boundaries of what you think you deserve, think bigger, stretch your mind beyond whatever limitations you were handed as a child. The intention must also include a willingness to meet any resistance or fear that arises—the censors, nay-sayers, and frightened parts that sabotage our actions. "I will not let irrational fear control me" is a helpful vow to take.

Setting an intention is like casting out a line and seeing where it takes you. In other words, be open to surprises. Often when we start down one path a more intriguing one presents itself and we do well to change course.

4. Gather information: open up, reach out, talk to people, research the situation, and explore all possibilities.

> *Creative thinking requires an outlook that allows you to search for ideas, and play with your knowledge and experience. You use crazy, foolish, and impractical ideas as stepping stones to practical new ideas. You break the rules occasionally, and explore for ideas in unusual outside places.*
> —ROGER VON OECH, *A WHACK ON THE SIDE OF THE HEAD*

At this stage you ask yourself, "What are the possibilities? What do I need to do? What do I need to let go of? How do I gather information? Who can I talk to? Who has faced a similar situation?" You can go to libraries, read books, look on the internet, and again, *talk with people*. Put out your antenna in all directions. So often the Buddha is just around the corner waiting to help you if you'll only open your eyes. She may be the woman standing at the check-out counter, your child's school teacher, your office assistant, your neighbor, or she may be sitting next to you on a bus.

Brainstorm various possibilities or solutions no matter how improbable or unlikely. It's far better to have lots of options to choose from than a single plan. Keep opening your imagination and your perceptions of the problem or task. If getting exercise is your intention, do you need to go to an exercise class regularly, get your bike tuned up, or find a friend to walk with or a pool to swim in? What's realistic, what feels easiest to do first?

Think big. Keep the possibilities open and flowing. And remember to stay away from nay-sayers and negative people who throw up obstacles. Fending off their negativity can drain your energy.

5. Make plans. This is where you say out loud, "It's decided. I'm going to do this. Here's my list and my schedule. This is what I'm going to do to eat better, exercise, be kinder to my family, be more diligent in my work, take time off, start looking for a new job, find someone to date," and so on. It may be a one-time plan like signing up for a workshop or a change that requires a series of steps.

Make a list of *everything* that needs to be taken care of. With exercise, for example, do you have a routine, a video, a place to walk, a mini-trampoline, weights, an aikido program? Do you belong to a fitness center? Do you have their schedule, a bathing suit if you're going to swim? When will you need to get up in the morning to exercise? (And when will you need to go to bed?) Work out *all* the details. And again, make dates with yourself on your calendar to get things done.

6. Remember, repetition is the mother of learning. You don't become relaxed about jumping off a high diving board through analyzing, insight, or listing all the reasons why it's scary. You jump! fear and all, then do it fifty more times. You recondition your brain and nervous system to realize, "I can jump off this high board, I will be all right, and nothing terrible is going to happen. Even if I get a little smack on my butt, I'll survive."

Albert Ellis, founder of Rational Emotive Therapy and author of *How to Stubbornly Refuse to Make Yourself Miserable About Anything*, writes about pushing himself to overcome his irrational fears. At one point in his young life, to overcome his fear of rejection by women, he gave himself the assignment of talking to every young woman he met sitting on one of the park benches on his daily walks. "No exceptions! No cop-outs." Out of the one hundred women he talked with, only one woman made a date with him, but he completely overcame his fear because he saw that nothing terrible happened if he was rejected.

Accept help. You may not always be able to motivate yourself to get started or take on a project. A good way you calm yourself and take the anxiety out of a project is getting a friend to help you. I am a lover of temp agencies for everything from planting daffodils to getting organized. For example, I was totally stuck cleaning out the basement, so for a birthday present to myself I called a temp agency and asked them for someone who was good at throwing stuff away. The "throwing stuff away" woman, who had just moved to town to start graduate school, took the job on a lark and, in addition to a clean basement, I gained a new friend.

If one approach doesn't work, try something else. If you have a change of heart, or a new possibility presents itself, or the plan is not feasible, you can drop it or change it. The point is to stay in forward motion.

7. Take action! At this point the dream, whether large or small, has become reality, you become a bit more congruent internally, and you experience yourself living more in the flow of your life. You've taken a morning walk three times in the last week, started the book group, bought the land, signed up for that class, invited your sweetie out on a date, attended your first Weight Watchers meeting.

Each clear step that expresses heart, mind, and body will stimulate your energy. You're on the upswing. Big changes may also leave you feeling a bit disoriented. It might take a while for your inside world to catch up to your new behavior or situation. "Am I really living in this new house?" "Do I actually have this good job?" "Am I really losing weight? Exercising?" "Is this me?" "Do I deserve this?" A friend of mine had repeated dreams of smoking after he quit; another had dreams about getting a letter that her Ph.D. had been cancelled.

Change inherently includes going toward one possibility and closing the door on others. Moving to start a great job might mean being away from your family. The park ranger who gets a higher position misses being outside. Being promoted to store manager means losing the peer camaraderie of fellow employees. Having a child brings joy *and* sleepless nights. You love your daily exercise but miss sitting with a cup of tea and reading the paper. That's the dance. Hello and goodbye all come together.

8. Persevere. If you fall off the horse get back on and keep riding. This is a crucial step. It's like keeping the weight off after you start a diet, continuing to take steps to meet a new partner, or playing more with your children. Don't lose heart if you start backtracking from the changes you are making. Most people fall off and get up many times before a new behavior is incorporated into their way of living. I was unable to finish a manuscript or article for over ten years before I finally completed one—a four hundred page book. I was watching the world figure skating competition and a Chinese skater said she fell forty-four times before she was able to land a quadruple jump. It was agonizing to see the videos of her falls . . . but beautiful to see the first time she made it—the joy radiated on her face. People who stay unstuck are good at getting back on the horse. It's not that anything is magically easy. They struggle, make mistakes, feel challenged, take a few spills, *and* keep going.

Staying aware of those sneaky little thoughts that grab you by the throat is a key to knowing yourself more deeply. Because action brings resistance to the surface, you learn to stare your saboteurs in the face. To meet your saboteurs, dance with them, and realize they are paper dragons from childhood will help lessen their power. It's like saying, "I'm not going to let a scared/needy little kid run my life. I'm an adult and I'm taking charge, even if I have to drag myself kicking and screaming to get started." Once you've taken these steps you can relax into the pleasure of being more comfortably centered in your life. Then take on something new.

46. Release Yourself of Roadblocks and Negative Thinking

In one Buddhist meditation practice, whenever the mind starts to wander you say "thinking" and come back to following your breath. You don't explore the thought or what it means; you see it generically as a thought and shift your focus back to your breathing.

You can do the same when your mind throws up a roadblock to change. Take note of any excuses, fears, complaints, negative thinking, or worries that are habitual and irrational. Instead of giving them mental attention, say "roadblock!" This is not to say that there aren't some realistic considerations to weigh when you make a decision, but it's habitual for people who stay stuck to think immediately about why something is hard or it won't work. It's like constantly throwing ice cubes in a soup you're trying to heat up. It's all about fear, usually of dissolving your ego's definition of who you are:

After saying "roadblock," ask yourself.

1. "What am I afraid of?" or "What am I resisting?"

2. "What's the worst thing about that?" As fear comes up, repeat the question until you get to the core of the fear.

3. "What if I didn't have that negative thought? What would happen if that belief simply evaporated, formless and harmless, into the universe, zapped by some cosmic laser beam?"

You can explore negative thinking from many perspectives. From a psychological perspective, it can be related to depression and be seen as a reflection of fear. From a Zen perspective, thoughts are just energy, you simply see the thought as a thought and not give it attention. From the Buddhist perspective in which we are not understood as individual selves nor with a separate lifespan, thinking is highly unimportant. And from the Buddhist perspective that we create our suffering through our attachments, you could look behind each negative thought for the underlying attachment, and ask, "What am I demanding be different than it is?" For example, if I say, "This damn fridge is falling apart," I might uncover a whole list of underlying demands—that the fridge work, that I have enough money to buy a new one, that my partner have fixed it when he said he would, and so on. This way we can use our negative thinking to see how we create our suffering.

As I've mentioned earlier, the primary purpose of this book is to work on the preparatory steps toward the ultimate level in Buddhism, which is letting go of the separate self, or individual identity, so you dwell in the flow of life. Thus, our exploration focuses on how negativity keeps us self-absorbed, locked into the ego, and creates suffering. The point is to notice the connections between our thinking and being stuck . . . or unstuck.

For many, negativity is a chronic interpretation of the world that reflects an inner sense of helplessness and despair. "The world is a mess." "You can never get anywhere." "Everyone is an incompetent idiot." "I might as well drink, scream at the kids, or spend all my money. Tomorrow may never come anyhow." These are some catchphrases that are learned in families where constant complaining and blaming are habitual.

I spoke with Maggie, who had been through numerous substance abuse treatment programs with only intermittent success. She said that visiting her family usually triggered a desire to drink or smoke. I asked her to describe what family visits were like. "Oh, they sit around and talk about the banks cheating us, and the poor getting ripped off, and how you can't trust anyone, and how nobody really cares, how stupid the neighbors are, and how it's a waste of money to have policemen anyhow, they never help. Sometimes they eat a lot or smoke dope and just sit around."

I asked Maggie what kinds of thoughts went through her head as a result. "Well, it used to be exactly the same as my family. I thought life was hopeless, so why not drink. Then in treatment I heard people making plans for their lives, having fun, being nice to each other, and helping each other to get on track. It felt really good, but it's hard for me to hang onto." As Maggie eventually realized, "The only way to be with my family was to be negative. If I was optimistic or said something nice about a friend they'd laugh at me or mock me, as if I was getting soft. I've had to stay away, which is hard."

If you have a chronic negativity habit, notice how it affects your mood, body, and motivation to make changes. When you're gloomy and depressed, the cells, bones, hormones, blood, and muscles in your body are depressed, and so is your immune system. When you have a positive outlook, your cells, bones, hormones, blood, muscles and immune system are given an infusion of energy.

Sometimes external stimulus leads to negativity. One friend said, "I've got to stop watching three hours of violent mysteries a night because I'm always dragged down in the morning." Notice by contrast what happens when you read an uplifting book—and I don't mean plastic happiness—I mean an account of someone who has shown grit and creativity and has taken positive action in their life. It's one thing to watch a historical movie that has a positive message, such as *Schindler's List,* and quite another to watch fast-moving violence with no social context or meaning.

While for the most part I have mostly spoken of being with whatever happens inside, when it comes to negative thinking you sometimes need to interrupt it to stop it from becoming an endless downward spiral. One psychological approach is to interrupt negative thoughts immediately and replace them with something else—take a small action, be grateful for what you do have, sing a song, recite a verse or poem, say a prayer, get up and move around—whatever stops the downward spiral. You need to send a message to the nervous system of "I'm not going there anymore." A naturopath or kinesiologist can help work with biochemical imbalances in the body that lower resistance to negative thinking. Feeling physically well often goes together with more positive thinking.

Most people I've interviewed who tend to stay unstuck avoid negative energy and whatever deflates or dulls their energy. At the same time, they don't hide from human suffering in the world.

Giving up chronic negativity or anger is akin to giving up an addictive substance—you might find a feeling of emptiness and depression underneath. It takes courage to risk this journey and we usually need companions at our side, whether it be a support group, good friends, a psychotherapist, or community.

Gratitude, which creates a high vibration of energy, is a powerful way to move through negativity. I don't want this to sound saccharine, because it's not. Gratitude opens us to a bigger world view. When we remember to be thankful that we can see, walk, have enough to eat, a bed, a heated home, friends, family, indoor plumbing, and access to education, and in turn be aware of those who live without clean water, shelter, and safety, and with a fraction of the opportunities we have, we may stop being so self-absorbed. In turn our vision can expand to take in the wonders of creation—to appreciate the chirping of a bird, the taste of a ripe peach, the opening of a leaf, a child's smile, a warm body nestled with ours—is manna to every cell and fiber of our being.

Here's a story that illustrates the power of seeing the beauty in creation: on a recent canoe and camping trip most of us were awakened, some with obvious irritation, by a very active woodpecker. A little while later my friend David emerged from his tent smiling and with perfect accuracy reproduced the phrase, rhythm, and cadences of the woodpecker's morning ritual. "If my son Matthew were here he'd turn it into a drum piece," he said. David brought a sense of freshness and delight to the situation that most of us had overlooked—same event, different experience.

47. Feel the Power of Resisting Your Impulses

There is great power in being able to let your sudden impulses pass through without acting on them. A quiet joy emerges when you find the deeper peace of staying steady in the face of external glitz, stimulation, and sense desires. This is difficult to do in a culture in which every store, every ad or commercial is arranged to pull at your impulses and get you to believe you really need all kinds of stuff to be fulfilled, attractive, or happy. We are seduced daily with images of sweeter, bigger, better, sexier, classier, more attractive, or lots of snazzy new features. Following an impulse unaccompanied by reason when getting into a new relationship after having had several catastrophes can result in yet another painful story.

Being able to resist impulses has long-reaching effects according to Walter Mischel's "marshmallow study," as described by Daniel Goleman in *Emotional Intelligence.* In the study four-year-old children were given the option of having one marshmallow immediately or having two if they could wait while the person administering the study "took a few minutes to run an errand." The children were then left alone in a room with the marshmallow on the table. Those who were able to wait for the two-marshmallow reward struggled hard— they would cover their eyes, rest their heads in their arms, talk to themselves, play games with their hands and feet, and even try to go to sleep. The ones who grabbed the one marshmallow did so almost immediately. Fourteen years later, there were striking differences between the "grab the marshmallow group" and the plucky kids who were able to restrain themselves for fifteen minutes.

According to Goleman, "Those who had resisted temptation at four were now, as adolescents, more socially competent: personally effective, self-assertive, and better able to cope with the frustrations of life. They were less likely to go to pieces, freeze, regress under stress, or become rattled and disorganized when pressured. They embraced challenges and pursued them instead of giving up even in the face of difficulties, they were self-reliant and confident."

This is a testimony to the power of our early conditioning and how important it is for parents to help their children learn restraint and control. It doesn't mean curtailing creativity; it means learning to think ahead and postpone gratification if it leads you to something better. If we didn't get this training in childhood, we can start now.

I want to distinguish between doing something quickly and being impulsive. You may have been planning to make a major change and a way suddenly opens, so you immediately follow it. It may look impulsive to people who don't know it's part of your plan, but it's really more about seizing the opportunity than being impulsive. Making a grounded but rapid decision reflects a stable interior world that allows you to make a big shift with reasonable certainty along with the confidence that you'll be all right no matter what the outcome.

48. Eat, Exercise, Be Merry, and Get Enough Sleep: The Wonder Drugs for Feeling More at Ease

First perfect your instrument. Then just play.
—CHARLIE PARKER

In my interviews many people have commented on the energizing impact of exercise and healthy eating: "I can be dragging around after work, but if I go to the gym for an hour, I feel great afterward and have energy to do something in the evening." Or "I am amazed over and over at how a brisk walk uphill in the morning lifts my mood and eases all my worries." And "My moods are directly related to how I eat, combined with exercise. If I keep it simple—lots of veggies and a little protein—I feel great. If I start on the sugar and white flour my head gets hazy, and then I want chocolate or stimulants." Our moods, perspective, and emotional states are directly related to the chemistry in the brain, which is greatly affected by exercise, restorative sleep, and healthy eating.

One caveat: from a Buddhist perspective, we don't want to get attached to a given state or think that it's morally better or worse to eat tofu and green beans than ice cream and fudge. Rather, we look at creating health in the body in relation to mindfulness and equanimity. A peaceful body helps us focus, concentrate, and bring a meditative mindset to whatever we are doing.

If we're constantly stimulating our adrenaline and nervous systems with sugar, alcohol, drugs, nicotine, and caffeine, we feel jumpy inside because the body is intermittently going in and out of withdrawal. We feel restless and can become obsessed with seeking a fix to quell our physical discomfort.

Thus the commitment to exercise, eat well, and get enough sleep is not just about *doing* something or being good to yourself; it's about a deep commitment to leading a mindful life—to creating the music of your existence. This is why the steps on the Buddha's Eightfold Path always had the prefix "right," as in right mindfulness, right concentration, and right effort.

Lama Surya Das, in *Awakening the Buddha Within*, explains the Dzogchen view of effort: "Dzogchen is beyond effort—not something to do, but a way of being." Referring to Charlie Parker's words, we want to practice our instrument well so we can just play. If we think of healthy eating, getting enough sleep, and exercising as a *way of being*, not just a task or a "should," it becomes intertwined with the whole of our spiritual journey. We need to move from a "should" exercise attitude to mindfulness of how our physical habits affect our emotional and mental ability to be at ease.

Remember the high from falling in love—how the world looked beautiful, the sky a gorgeous blue, the breeze a tender caress, and you were immensely forgiving of people's inadequacies? The same hormonal bath that created that sense of well-being also functions in relation to being rested, getting exercise, eating well, being passionate about what you are doing, appreciating beauty, and having loving connections in your life.

It's incredibly hard for many people to believe that they have within them the power to affect their health and well-being dramatically by their own daily actions. When I ask people in my workshops across the country to name their New Year's resolutions it's always get more exercise, lose weight, eat better, and do more of what I enjoy in life. Of course we make resolutions because cultivating new habits feels like an insurmountable challenge.

I know that exercise, getting sleep, and eating well can sound like a boring cliché. It's such an unglamorous aspect of taking action—no pills, fancy trips, or excelling at something. But it's like fine-tuning the instrument of your body and spirit so, again, as Charlie Parker said, you can "just play." Many people have overcome long-term back pain with yoga; others have healed from depression with exercise, diet, and finding work they enjoyed. Most of all, your heart—the pulse beat of your life—thrives on exercise, healthy eating, loving connections, and rest.

We know that if there were a pill that could lower blood pressure, help maintain bone density, improve our circulation, digestion, breathing, blood flow, energy level, metabolism, flexibility, sleep, and ability to learn, boost our immune system, and improve our mental outlook with no side effects, everyone would want it. But they don't take it. You know the answer. It's called a thirty- to sixty-minute period of moderate to intense exercise four or five times a week—brisk walking, biking, swimming, weight training, martial arts, aerobic workouts—along with stretching or yoga to keep the body flexible. It's also about eating the right amount of fresh fruits, vegetables, protein, and grains to resonate with your particular body and blood type, and less sugar, refined foods, and artificial anything. Why is it so hard? Several reasons come to mind. It takes effort, pushes at our comfort zone, and means giving up short-term gratification. It also may mean cracking through our sense of deservedness or limiting thoughts such as "That's what other people do," or "I can't believe my life could be different."

Notice connections. You can deepen your awareness and hopefully your motivation when you notice the connection between diet/substances, exercise, rest, and and your ability to concentrate, stay healthy, focus, and be energetic. Our eating or exercise habits can create a domino chain. For example, getting hooked on sugar and caffeine to the exclusion of healthy food can make you restless, cause your blood sugar to drop, break your concentration, lower your energy, cause you to feel irritated with others, and lead to needing more sugar and caffeine to stave off feelings of lethargy. Eventually it can lead to illness.

As a starting place, do something small. It's better to do a relatively short, easy walk, add greens to your diet, and keep at it even after you've missed a few days than to start with super-high goals that fade away. Said another way, it's better to be steady over the long haul than spectacular for a few weeks. While lack of self-care has some direct relationship to the intensity of our false core beliefs—believing deeply that you are worthless, powerless, and a loser—in looking through my interview notes I've found that that's not the whole story. People who do get into healthy exercise, eating, and sleeping routines tend to be able to mobilize themselves in spite of false core beliefs. Here are some shared experiences:

On Health Clubs

I asked some women in the locker room, "How do you get yourself here?"

"I can't get here on my own, so I take a water aerobics class. I need the peer pressure—I don't want to hear people saying, 'hey, where were you?'"

"I never came on my own so I hired a personal trainer—this way I know I'll show up."

"I meet a friend at 6:45 a.m. and I'd be too embarrassed to call and wake up her husband to cancel, so I just get here."

"My husband and I come together, so there's always one of us to say, 'come on, let's go,' if the other is feeling lazy. It's a wonderful way to be together. Also . . . it's great for our sex lives."

"It's not hard; I just love coming. But if I'm tired, I tell myself I don't need to force myself—just do something—maybe walk a mile and do some biking and a few weights. Even if I only do forty minutes, I always feel better."

At Home and Outside

"I meet a friend four times a week to walk four miles."

"I bought some videos—a tae-bo tape and others on yoga, and a couple on aerobics. They sat around for a long time—then I got one out and actually did it. I have a little trampoline, some weights, and an exercycle. When I wake up in the morning I scan my choices and do whatever feels good."

"I bought a little jogger, and my rule is that if I'm going to watch TV, I have to use the jogger for at least a half hour."

Here's what women said in response to my question, "What keeps you exercising regularly?"

"I feel better," was the overall response that was reflected in many ways—I have more energy, feel brighter, my work goes better, I'm in a better mood.

Other responses:

"I don't want junk food afterward."

"It helps me keep my weight down."

"I don't want to get osteoporosis."

"It keeps me from getting depressed."

"I sleep better."

"Flat out," one woman said strongly, "I want to be healthy when I get older. I see so many people in my family sick. My aunt walks like this," she said, demonstrating the hunched-over stance. "I saw my mother clutching her chest with angina pains, and I saw my brother do the same."

Returning to the health club, I asked Bill at the front desk why he thought people worked out regularly.

"Fear," he said.

I was surprised.

"Fear of dying, fear of heart attacks. Many of the men started coming here after a heart attack. They want a better quality of life. I also think people like the positive atmosphere." He grinned. "They get to see me!"

I laughed with him. But it was true. There's something sweet about knowing I'll get a friendly greeting as I'm handed a fresh towel. It's a little like the Cheers bar. I see the same people on the track, exchange hellos, and have superficial chats. The women often have friendly conversations in the locker room about hormones, weight loss, families, work . . . just good-natured exchanges.

On the subject of sleep, I asked my friend Dodi how she maintained her amazing schedule and always seemed relaxed and friendly with three teenage daughters, a full-time job, and a weekend disco business with her husband, and then she's out biking and having fun. I never see her dragging around saying how tired she is.

She responded emphatically, "I always get enough sleep." Followed by, "I get a lot of exercise riding my bike (ten miles to and from work, up a three-mile hill) and we have a lot of fun as a family."

For some people, the issue of sleep isn't just about getting to bed early—it's about lowering anxiety so you can get to sleep, easing depression so you can stay asleep, and fostering a consciousness that eases worry. Worried minds don't rest well. For those with an autoimmune disease, sleep can be problematic as well. People have shared numerous strategies to help them relax into sleep, including taking amino acids, herbal remedies, reading in bed (nothing too exciting), drinking relaxing teas, self-massage, back rubs, listening to audio tapes, Reiki healing, getting a new mattress, or a satisfying love life.

To people who value sleep it becomes more important than old movies on TV, late-night phone conversations, cleaning, or fixing things. As one woman said to me, "The house is kind of sloppy and sometimes we wear day-old socks and eat simple meals, but exercise, relaxation, and sleep are at the top of my list."

In a myriad of ways your body tells the story of your life and cannot be separated from spirit. Relaxation, flexibility, strength, concentration, energy, joy, and being with the flow are intricately woven aspects of our being at every level.

49. Take on the Saboteurs

> *Progress is impossible without change, and those who cannot change their minds cannot change anything.*
> —RALPH WALDO EMERSON

> *We have met the enemy and it is us.*
> —POGO

I f you want your life to be *different, you have to do something different.* To do something different often means getting past a lifetime of conditioning and beliefs that grab you by the throat when you attempt to change your life. In other words, you can feel a bit like David meeting Goliath when you start in a positive direction. But instead of picking up a slingshot, we will approach these discouraging voices, critics, and censors with awareness.

We'll bring our mental habits and thought patterns on screen, where we we they can be seen, explored, and understood, and eventually transformed. I am indebted to Stephen Wolinsky for processes 2 and 4. I refer the reader to his books listed in the recommended readings at the back of this book, to learn about other processes.

The processes that follow are central to loosening your identity with your thoughts, beliefs, and concepts. It's about sorting out what's you from what's not you so you can give birth to your real self. You may find one that speaks to you, or you may want to try them all. Done repeatedly, they are likely to be very freeing.

Dismantling Your Censors and Saboteurs

EXERCISE 1.

Notice Your Sabotaging Thoughts or Behaviors

Whenever any of the thoughts on the following list come up, recognize them as the cunning, clever, and ingenious saboteur or censor within you. Notice how they discourage you from starting or completing tasks or dish out guilt when you take time to relax or take good care of yourself. Remember, they got into you through your conditioning but they are not who you really are. At the same time, don't fight them or give them energy—just be aware of them.

THOUGHTS

- You don't deserve it.
- You aren't worth it.
- Yeah, right—sure you can.
- You're a loser.
- It's hopeless.
- Who do you think you are?
- Let's wait until tomorrow.
- Danger! Those feelings will get you in trouble.
- You won't be loved if you do that.
- Don't be lazy; you should be productive.
- Excuses: There's not enough time. It would cost money. I don't know how.

EMOTIONS AND BODY SENSATIONS

- Fear, loneliness, sadness, anxiety, you might make a mistake, not look good to the world, not be productive, for example.
- Apathy or inertia—you want to go to bed and wake up when it's over.
- Distraction.

- Anxiety at the prospect of doing something new.
- Sleepiness at the prospect of doing something new.
- Tension in your body when you attempt something new.

Keep a daily journal of all the thoughts or experiences that signal your saboteur or censor is operating. Think of times when you started to to do something proactive for yourself then stopped.

EXERCISE 2.

Peel Back: What's Under Your Fears?

This is often known as checking for the worst case scenario. It is taught in therapy classes and is a common technique for bringing people into reality and letting go of old fears.

Take a situation where you feel afraid or stuck, are sabotaging yourself, or making excuses or giving reasons why you can't do something. Then peel it back by asking, "Then what?" Stephen's version is to ask, "What's the worst thing about that?" Use whatever works for you.

For example:

> *I'm really afraid to leave this relationship.*
> What's the worst thing about that?
> *I'd be alone.*
> What's the worst thing about that?
> *I'd be scared.*
> What's the worst thing about that?
> *I'd get depressed.*
> What's the worst thing about that?
> *I might kill myself.*
> What's the worst thing about that?
> *I'd be dead.*

At this point, people often smile or laugh, because they realize they probably will not die and that it's not a cosmic catastrophe.

Use Affirmations to Flush Out Your Saboteurs

This form of affirmation is to flush out censors and saboteurs so you are aware of them. You choose a possibility or an action you would like to take, and see what arguments or sabotaging thoughts come up. Choose one affirmation (for example, *I can start exercising*), then listen to whatever argument comes up. Allow one argument per affirmation.

For example:

I can start exercising regularly.
Oh, sure. You never have before.
I can start exercising regularly.
You'd have to give up the late show.

- Choose an affirmation that opens up a possibility. You can use one of the following or make up your own.
  I can _____.
  I will not let fear stop me from _____.
  I can take care of myself by _____.
  I can love myself by _____.
  I can improve my life by _____.
- Keep saying the affirmation until all arguments subside. This may require weeks, or even months. Even if the argument fades on a given day, come back to the affirmation several times to check for any other internalized messages that may be getting in your way.
- Repeat daily (or as often as possible) until you feel an internal shift.

Variation: Walk or jog while saying or thinking the affirmation; use a lap counter to click with each of the above-mentioned affirmation.

Notes: Don't quit when the opposition mounts. As you are getting close to a shift, you may feel an incredible force pushing back at you. Just keep going. (I did this to write my first book.)

EXERCISE 4.

In-Depth Exploration of Stuck Places

This is a modified version of a process Stephen Wolinsky teaches in his introductory workshop. It is the basic exercise used to dismantle false core beliefs.

Choose a pair of beliefs to dismantle, such as "I am worthless" and "I am worthwhile." Then go through a detailed list of questions to investigate how they operate in your life. Do one first and then the other. The purpose is to stop false core beliefs from operating unconsciously so you can fully grasp their impact on your life. This usually de-energizes your false core beliefs so they ultimately lose their power.

If you are doing this process in a dyad, one person asks the questions and the other responds, saying everything that comes to mind without going off into long stories. It works best if both people drop down into their bodies as they pose the question or give the answer.

Note: Skip any questions that don't seem relevant. Add or subtract questions as you see fit, but let the reponder have this list of the questions so he can let you know if you skipped something that seems important.

The questions:

- Who modeled this behavior/concept _____?
- Where in your body do you experience this concept _____?

- What have been the consequences of this belief _____?
- Go through the following questions, always repeating the first part, Have you ever used this belief _____ (of being worthless) to:

Get taken care of?

Avoid anything?

Bond with others?

Get sympathy?

Stay in a painful relationship?

Reinforce feeling helpless?

Blame others?

Maintain an image of yourself (good, mellow, loser, nice, important, insecure)?

Give yourself an identity or feel important or significant?

Feel special?

Feel superior or inferior or both?

Punish anyone? Including yourself?

Prove yourself to someone?

Keep someone from leaving you?

Have fantasies of the future when you will have what you want?

Avoid taking care of your health?

Avoid doing something hard?

Feel special or different?

Avoid feeling anxious?

Cover up feelings of fear?

Cover up feeling lonely?

Cover up feeling angry?

Cover up beliefs of being _____? (inadequate, worthless, invisible, powerless, or helpless)

Allow yourself to overwork?

Avoid managing your finances?

Justify ruthless behavior?

Justify addictive behavior?

Avoid taking responsibility?

Not succeed beyond a family member or outshine others?

Stay loyal or connected to someone?

Anything else?

- Was there any shocking, disturbing, or chaotic event that occurred prior to taking on this belief?
- When you took on this belief was there anything you pretended not to see, understand, or know? Were there any other beliefs that got created?

- Now imagine this thought_____ as just a thought or concept that got created, then think of it as energy.
- See yourself and the thought floating in an empty space. Then notice how you and the thought and the empty space are made of the same energy. Notice how you feel in your body.
- Ask yourself, "What do you want more than anything else?"

50. Seventeen Strategies for Staying on Track

Taking action is a major challenge along the journey to getting unstuck. An even greater challenge is to keep on track, which often includes a struggle with our mounting inner resistance or our saboteurs. In the previous chapter we talked about dismantling them; in this chapter we'll talk about how to dance around them.

Here's what appears to happen internally: picture yourself with two parts inside—the "real you" who wants to make a change and the ego/saboteur who is afraid of change. When you start a new endeavor like taking time to relax, eating well, getting exercise, speaking more gently to your children, the ego isn't worried at first; it thinks it's just fun and games. The first few weeks often go well. But as you persevere, the ego's existence is threatened. So the ego/saboteur mounts a counterattack—it sneaks up on you, causing you to get distracted, bored, make rationalizations, and say, "Oh, what the heck, it's not that important." *This is when you need to persevere no matter what!* You need to develop strategies and do whatever it takes to keep going. Eventually, if you persist, the ego resistance will ease and the new habit will become part of you.

Here is a list developed from interviews with people who manage to complete tasks or creative endeavors and keep up with projects of all sorts, including self-care, opening up in a relationship, and new endeavors.

1. Do not demand perfection.

Slips and slides are not the problem. Giving up is the problem. Just keep going back, again and again and again. A few moments of relaxation and conscious breathing are better than none; an apple is better than a Twinkie; clearing out one stack of clutter gives you one clear surface and some breathing room in your dwelling place. *Remember, it's better to do something fairly well over the long haul than to be perfect for a short time and then quit all together.*

2. Have realistic expectations, be flexible, and start with small goals.

Don't set yourself up for failure. Don't take on fixing up the whole house, hiking five miles a day, or eating perfectly. Make a list of little projects and be realistic about how long they each take. Allow a lot of latitude so you don't build up resistance. Floss half your teeth. Sweep half the floor. Walk up the stairs a little faster. You want to sneak past your ego resistance a little bit at a time without mounting a head-on collision.

3. Develop strategies to make life easier.

For example, if you're trying to eat better, you might clear out the junk food, buy healthy prepackaged foods (washed salad greens or bags of cut up clean vegetables, or grated cheese), make a soup or a big pot of something good for several days, and freeze quarts of it to have handy.

4. Start with whatever is easiest.

Scan your list of things to do and see which one seems easiest to start with. If you always proceed to the next easiest step, none will be so difficult.

5. Get help from a friend or be near other people.

Sometimes it's daunting to take on even a simple task alone. For many people it echoes a place inside that was alone and overwhelmed far too much as a child. It can be incredibly comforting to have a friendly face, a helping hand, some know-how to get the job done—from clearing out a closet, to taking a walk, to applying for a new job. Likewise, if you feel isolated, you can go to a library or bookstore that offers comfortable chairs to sit and read. You can take a walk where you'll be near others. While solitude is restful, isolation tends to dull us.

6. Change the setting.

I know several writers (including me) who go to a café to read over their manuscripts just to have a change of scene. If one setting pales, for anything from exercise, eating, walking, or meeting a friend, think of something that might be more appealing. Change the furniture around in your house. Move the pictures. Be as creative as possible.

7. Hire someone.

Okay, so you've tried to make a repair, balance your checkbook, fix a leaky faucet, get some little task done, and all you have to show for it six months later is a lot of guilt, anxiety, and stress. It can be a great relief to hire someone to help. In other words, give yourself a break—most of us have some areas of our lives that make us want to run for cover. You get to be good at some things and a lot less competent at others. If you can't afford to hire someone, find someone to swap with.

8. Give yourself rewards.

Some people think the concept of rewards sound silly, something like when we were children and got little star stickers for doing our chores. But adults like rewards too; getting them taps into the child in us. At Weight Watchers they give "bravo" star rewards for everything—losing five pounds, showing up sixteen times, gaining weight and not quitting the program. Think of what would feel good to you.

9. Readjust your goals.

If you repeatedly don't meet your goals, readjust them so they are realistic and possible. You're likely to stay with something when it gives you a feeling of mastery and success. Set yourself up for success, not guilt and recriminations.

10. Do something for a given time period every day.

This step is for people who are afraid of starting something because they feel powerless to stop. This could be sorting boxes, writing, playing music, cleaning, or taking on a task. Set some kind of limit—one hour, one box, and do no more or no less. Doing this can help you develop internal control. You can learn a great deal about yourself from noticing what happens when you stick to a schedule or set a limit.

11. Stay focused on the big picture.

The big picture is your life—your happiness, health, and well-being and the mysterious nature of life. You are becoming more of who you truly are (or who you are not) and are getting closer to your essence when you get all the distractions of guilt, clutter, and a speeding mind cleared out. This allows you to hear the silence, to drift with the flow of impermanence.

12. Make appointments on your calendar.

I've referred to this earlier, but it's important enough to include here again. If you have difficulty sticking to a plan, schedule times to exercise, study, clean, do yoga, then write them in your appointment book. Think of this as having a date with a very important person in your life—you.

13. Hang out with your resistance.

Notice anxiety, physical sensations, breathing difficulty, numbing out, rationalizing. Just sit and be with them and ask, "What is this about? What false core belief is underneath this?" Notice any shame, guilt, or ego-driven thoughts, and remind yourself this is about the temporal rise and fall of sensations and thoughts but not about the essential aliveness that is constant.

14. Give yourself a whack (not physical).

Sometimes we need to be jarred loose. Mary, who was pining for a lost love, said that a friend jarred her loose when she exclaimed, "Just let him go! Just send him down the river! Say good-bye. Put him in a barge and let him go. Don't keep talking about him." This may sound perilously close to, "Just say no." But sometimes we need to say, "Enough, I'm not going there any more. That's it. I'm going to listen to my wise mind." We need to give ourselves a little lecture and make a commitment to shift our focus. It's important to exert mental discipline and not indulge our misery and melancholic gloom.

15. Take one extra step.

This step is for expanding the boundaries of your perceived capacity and ability. It's about getting past the resistant ego by doing just a bit more than you set out to. If you say you're going to swim twenty laps, swim twenty-one. If you're taking a walk, go one extra block. If you keep nudging yourself past your perceived limitations, you will develop a sense of greater inner strength. Of course some people need to do the opposite—to let their body tell them its time to quit pushing themselves and stop.

16. Do it anyhow—anxiety and all.

When you take action, shake loose, and attempt something new, it often brings up feelings of uneasiness. If you learn to take action while tolerating ripples of fear, a fuzzy brain, or anxiety pulling on you, you will keep going forward. Persevering in this way can deepen a sense of confidence and competence. Remember, nearly every action gets easier with repetition—from the first kiss, to using an electric sander, to cooking spaghetti.

17. Lighten up.

Remember, in the big picture it all matters—but it's not serious. Whether you keep moving down the track, sit by the roadside, or even have your feet stuck in mud, it is just where you are at this moment—nothing is better or worse—it's all part of the big cosmic dance, the One Energy. We take the steps to lower stress and bring ease to our lives so we can have more clarity of mind and peacefulness of body. Make your best effort, and watch the unfolding drama.

Imagine flying up in the sky and looking down at homes, hospitals, prisons, office buildings, bars, and movie theaters and watch the unfolding dramas of so many lives, very similar to yours. Not on the surface, perhaps, but at the heart everyone wants to be free of suffering, be cared for, know happiness, and find some form of peace. Above all, be kind and merciful with yourself.

STEP SEVEN

Let Go

> *I teach one thing and one thing only:*
> *Suffering and the end of suffering.*
> —THE BUDDHA

Let Go

51. Welcome Home

We have come to the final stage of our journey—letting go. It's the ultimate step toward ending our suffering in which we feel an abiding happiness—a spacious, relaxed mind, body, and spirit, and a feeling of living in the heart of life. It doesn't mean life is always easy, rather that we stop fighting against our experience and accept the natural changes and losses that life inevitably brings. Letting go is built on all of the steps that have come before: remembering to show up for life, step back from your minds, enter into your experience, reach out to others, live in reality, and commit to action that frees you.

We become unstuck when we cease grasping at that which is temporal—our minds, bodies, situations, and lifespan. We rest in the deeper awareness that life exists in the "I Am" and the unified field of One Indivisible Energy where we started from on this journey.

Stephen Wolinsky told the following story at one of his workshops; he called it "Go Back the Way You Came." A young man traveled by boat from Europe to India seeking relief from his misery and disgust with himself. He asked the Indian guru Ramana Maharshi for advice. Maharshi responded, "Go back the way you came." A longtime student who overheard his remark said, "That was mean. How can you tell him that, after he came all this way here to get your help?" Maharshi responded, "I meant it. Not to go back to Europe, but to go back to the beginning of that thought and ask, 'From where did that thought arise?'" In other words, go back to that place in you that existed before your mind had thoughts.

To go back the way you came is to retrace your steps from your false core beliefs and compensating patterns of proving the impossible, namely that you are good, worthwhile, and lovable or bad, worthless, and unlovable to drop beneath your thoughts into the emptiness and quiet of "I Am." You explore all the ways you got sidetracked and keep asking yourself, is my approach to life working? Are my beliefs and actions helping me feel at ease in the world or putting me on a treadmill?

You drop back to the time prior to taking on concepts and beliefs when you were free to resonate, touch, sense, and take delight in simple things with an open, relaxed mind. There is now, this moment, this feeling, this amazing breath, this mystery of creation. To return to the "I Am," you give up the game of searching for a special answer, magic moments, or the seven secrets of enlightenment. Going toward freedom is to dismantle what's in the way rather than looking for an answer outside yourself.

When Siddhartha Gautama left the ascetics he had come to the conclusion that the drunk in the bar and the one obsessed with severe asceticism were not so far apart. An obsession with either renunciation or alcohol is a compulsion and a distraction from the crucial questions that inherently lie within: what is the nature of the mind, of being, of existence?

One of Nisargadatta's students asked, "There are so many theories about man and the universe. . . . Which are true?"

Nisargadatta answered:

All are true, all are false. You can pick up whichever you like best. Theories are neither right nor wrong. They are attempts at explaining the inexplicable . . . it is the testing of the theory that makes it fruitful. *It is the earnestness that liberates and not the theory.*

Letting go is a daily practice based on your earnest desire for freedom from identifying with your thoughts and your identity. To let go you observe the rising and falling of thoughts and emotions—you learn to be be aware of them but not immersed in them. If a concept of being good, bad, smart, or stupid arises, you become able to see it like the smoke and mirrors of the Wizard of Oz—a little man behind a curtain pulling levers and creating an illusion.

Another part of letting go is to slow down and make friends with whatever feelings and emotions arise—neither making a story out of them, forcing their expression, nor pushing them away away. You just stay with them and let them unwind. In many ways letting go is to let go of holding back, of running away; it's about staying connected, opening up, being real, and dropping all the masks. When you can let someone see your tears, your hurt, your sadness, your beauty, you naturally enter the flow of loving, giving, receiving. The heart opens, the body becomes resonant.

52. What Is This Feeling of Emptiness? Notice the Withdrawal Symptoms of Letting Go

The teachings I give you are a raft.
—THE BUDDHA

Letting go creates a wonderful image. It is the way toward love, contentment, and breaking free. To get a visceral feeling of what letting go is like, put out your hands, palms up, make tight fists, and notice how this affects your whole body—your breathing, your jaw, your muscles. Then breathe out and let your fists fall open. Breathe again. Just as holding tightly puts the squeeze on every part of your body, letting go helps everything start to flow together.

The ego resists with all its might because letting go also means falling into the empty space beyond thoughts, concepts, images, and teachings. It can feel disorienting and unfamiliar—kind of like going through withdrawal from a substance. I will list the cues at the end of this chapter so you're aware of them if they occur.

When the Buddha said the teachings are a raft, he meant that you can use them to navigate from the land of unconsciousness to the other side of the river, which symbolizes being awake. When you reach the other side, you let go of the teachings and journey on, attuning, responding, and be-ing, instead of following the rules, teachings, or advice of others. Another image is that you climb onto your little raft to cross the river and halfway across it starts falling apart, the boards and sticks float away, and there you are in deep water with nothing to hang on to. You end up swimming all on your own—no rules, guidelines, or predictable answers. You have only yourself and the "what is" of the moment. You sink into the silence of just being. This is why it can be scary to let go.

Likewise, letting go means dropping the external trappings used to symbolize spirituality. There is no particular diet, clothing, icon, or daily ritual that provides a sure path to happiness or unhappiness. If you decide to become a vegetarian, wear black, shave your head, pray, throw the i ching, do tai chi, yoga, breathing exercises, or bow one hundred times a day, you do it without any agenda attached to it. It can be lovely to bow, to say namaste, or to meditate, but the minute you think it is a path to somewhere, you're hooked. There are no paths because we're not going anywhere. You can enjoy feeling healthy, vital, and alive without labeling it spiritual or not spiritual. The living is in being warm-hearted, alive, and friendly.

> *The Yogi comes along in his famous orange,*
> *but if inside he is colorless, then what?*
> *Mohammed pours over words and points out this and that,*
> *but if his heart is not soaked dark with love, then what?*
> —Kabir, *44 Ecstatic Poems of Kabir*

As soon as you have made a thought, laugh at it.
—LAO-TZU

When I think of letting go I have this image of an interior structure built over time—like a Structo set or a Tinkertoy—made up of thoughts, beliefs, and concepts that give me an anchor in life. Then, I imagine pulling out a crucial piece and letting the whole contraption collapse. No longer any clear beliefs, concepts, or sureness about anything. It's a groundless feeling. No anchor, no thought. You can see it in the ease with which children can knock over a sand castle they built because they aren't attached to the structure. It's all sand play—delving in the sand, building, creating, then knocking it all down. Adults tend to feel uneasy about this because we get attached to our creations.

Dismantling your concepts can feel like taking off your makeup, fancy clothes, titles, degrees, snazzy car, miseries, and wounds so you stand in the world without labels, without anything impressive, extraordinary, or valuable. As the Zen master who says, "I have nothing to lose because I have nothing," we start to feel the freedom of nothing to protect, hold on to, or identify with.

When you first begin to let go of your belief structures, be prepared for some withdrawal symptoms. They are common and natural. The idea is to notice them as a passing experience and not be alarmed or surprised or think you have made a mistake on your journey home. *Have them; observe them; take a deep breath.*

Here are some withdrawal symptoms from letting go:

- You feel disoriented, giddy, silly, uneasy. Without the familiar internal structures, you feel dazed, or not quite sure of who you are.
- You feel alienated because you no longer hold to the stories and structures of belief that are the center of many conversations. You wonder whether to say something or sit quietly. It's hard to know what to do until you drop into a deeper ease where guidance arises from within.

- Your ego makes you doubt yourself: "Who are you to be so different from everyone else! How can you drop these popular beliefs? You're just being difficult. Maybe you're wrong."
- You suddenly feel sad, angry, anxious, or sleepy. Again, dismantling our belief systems is a scary proposition to the ego.
- You have a sudden fear of being empty or falling into nothingness without your structures of belief. There's a sense of not having control.
- Your body feels rootless, unstable, or unfamiliar. That's because the framework created by your beliefs permeates your whole body, which will soften and relax as you let go of core beliefs about life, spirituality, and who you think you are. Some people fear they can't function without being rigid and tightly held. But you can. You feel a bit wobbly at first, but you actually find that flexibility and openness are easier.
- You have an empty-headed feeling that leaves you wondering if you can accomplish anything, or write, or be creative. But when you focus on what you want to do, it can feel like flipping a switch and having ideas pour in. It can feel like tapping into the great cosmic library of understanding and knowledge.

53. Welcome Emptiness and the Energy of the Unknown

Life is its own journey, presupposes its own change and movement, and one tries to arrest them at one's eternal peril.
—VACLAV HAVEL, VENTURE TO THE INTERIOR

We ease into an enormous spaciousness when we step beyond our conditioned self, cease the chatter in our minds, and relax into silence. Many people fear this open space and drown it out with chaos, frenetic activity, and constant noise. But it's always accessible, and it can be a wonderous place.

Emptiness is not vacuous—it is not the terrifying abyss children fear when they are left alone or ignored. Emptiness is the energy that forms the building blocks of the universe. To let go means to float in the emptiness or quiet within, a terrifying prospect to some. But, as Stephen Wolinsky teaches, if you imagine yourself floating in space, noticing your boundaries dissolving and realizing it's all one energy, this emptiness becomes restful and not like a frightening nothingness.

Allowing yourself to feel empty is akin to staying open on your journey so that something new can be born within you. Your role is to notice where your aliveness takes you and be a gracious host—even if it comes by surprise or in a series of unanticipated events, as was the case for Harold McCoy.

When Harold McCoy, born and raised in Arkansas, came back from twenty-five years of military service he was, in his words, a country redneck drinking twelve beers a day and smoking two packs of cigarettes. He settled back into a predictable life with his family and nearby relatives. He didn't know he was stuck because he was living the only life he knew, patterned after his culture, family, and the military social system.

Shortly after his return, Harold got involved with a group of dowsers* who had been family friends since his youth. This is how Harold described it: "The dowsing came naturally—every community had an old water witcher who helped people find where to dig a

---

*The idea behind dowsing, or water witching, is to locate underground water using a divining rod, which can be a forked stick or two wires, one held in each hand. You set an intention—I want to find a clear well—then walk through an area with a forked stick or two bent wires until the wires cross or the forked stick pulls downward when you are over the well. It is an age-old skill in which the person holding the divining rod becomes part of an electromagnetic field combining mental intention, mind, and the sought-after water.

well. I had seen it as a child, and I had found out I could do it too. Everyone believed that kind of stuff happened.

"The day I started the dowsing group was the first time I ever helped heal anyone. Thirty-one people had just arrived when my wife fell on a step and cracked her ankle. It got real swollen and was hurting her. Something led me to put my hands on that ankle and sit with her, and it was down to normal in a couple of hours. I was totally surprised. Something took over and I was just the conduit. I didn't know what the heck I was doing. I did it and it worked.

"I started experimenting with people's aches and pains and there was no lack of people wanting help. Eventually, I would close my eyes and start seeing images of someone's brain and where there was congestion or emotional pain, or things weren't attached properly. Then I'd have an image of a table beside me with the tools I'd need to connect the circuits, or clean out the rough places. It usually helped, and people started healing from all kinds of illnesses, so I kept on doing it, and pretty soon people wanted me to teach them. I feel I was picked to do this." He added, jokingly, "I just do what I'm told to do. I had good training for taking orders in the army. Now I take direction from a higher source."

Looking back now, as the founder and director of the Ozark Research Institute and traveling throughout the country to give weekend trainings on the the power of the mind to heal, he muses on the vast changes in his life. "Sometimes it seems like the powers that be are going to get you where they want, even if they have to hit you over the head to get you there. The universe kept trying to wake me up—I had something important to do."

Harold continued, "When you get your heart totally into something like this, it's amazing how it attracts other people. You wouldn't believe the gifts we've received and the help that's literally walked in the door."

I asked Harold what he believed to be helpful for those who wanted to expand their inner world and make change. "Partly, it's the luck of the draw. But people who get stuck are often pessimists and don't believe much of anything. You've got to understand that we don't understand anything, so you've got to be open. I know I work with a higher source. I think that's what we all do. You have to get over those limitations you put on yourself—get past the nay-sayers inside. So many people blame others and make up excuses. 'Someone broke my heart. I'm wounded.' Only you are responsible for your happiness. If you get in that mind-set, everything changes."

No more cigarettes and beer. Harold and his wife, Gladys, who also teaches workshops on healing, live a full life immersed in a devoted community of people who work with them. Harold takes no credit for the healings he "gives," nor does he take money for himself. The minimal charge goes back to the research institute. The friendliness and availability of both Harold and Gladys are common traits of people who have dissolved into their life's purpose and let go of being absorbed with their identity.

Harold's story follows some common threads involved in the process of getting unstuck and breaking free. Harold followed a strong impulse without questioning it, observed the results, was willing to proceed without knowing what he was doing, took no individual credit for what happened—"the powers that be get you where you need to go"—and let go of his self-image as a country redneck. He allowed himself to be astonished and changed and was willing to follow a new path.

54. Try Moving Toward a Vision Without a Map

I didn't make any mistakes,

I just know a thousand ways not to make a light bulb.

—THOMAS EDISON

I spoke with Piotr Blass, a mathematician, about emptiness: "Going into emptiness sometimes means you have an overall sense of something you could do, create, or understand. You see it in its entirety, maybe without words or any idea of how to get there, but you know it's where you want to go. It may take months or even years to fill in the details and you may go down a lot of blind alleys."

Glenn Miller, a young trombone player and arranger, had a passion for finding a certain sound that was different from anything he had ever heard in a jazz band. He had a sense of the sound but couldn't describe it. He spent years playing in different groups, studying arranging, and getting inklings of what he wanted. He finally arrived at his "sound" after his horn player cut his lip and Miller spent all night rewriting the arrangements with a clarinet player as soloist. He didn't realize he had found the sound until he heard the band play the next day.

Kristie, a friend and artist, also had a vision of something she wanted to see happen and went toward it without a map. Kristie had a studio overlooking the Berkeley Pit in Butte, Montana, an enormous gaping wound in the earth, the result of years of open-pit mining. A green liquid, akin to battery acid, was slowly seeping into the pit. Kristie, a woman with a quiet demeanor, loves to dance the hula. One day as she was gazing out the window of her studio she had an image of a group of people dancing the hula on the ridge above the pit. It struck her that this could be a way to bring something beautiful and soft to the barren, stripped land.

Inspired by her vision she started talking with anyone who showed an interest and made connections with the Montana women's chorus and various peace networks. Many times she was overcome by doubt, questioned herself, or wondered what she was doing. But she persevered, encouraged by the welcoming response she got from so many people: "Sure, I'll go to the Berkeley Pit and dance the hula." Just over a year later, on a beautiful Big Sky Montana day, 165 people dressed in bright blue skirts streamed single file onto the ridge and danced the hula to the song "Cool, Clear Water," with the media recording the event. Kristie brought attention to an ecological disaster through beauty, dancing, and playfulness rather than the usual angry rhetoric—she followed a vision. (See the Resources for an inspiring video of the event.)

We leap into knowing and not knowing all at once. If you sense a possibility but want all the details and guarantees of "success" in place before moving forward, you may never move to action. You often have to take a first step before the next one presents itself. You break free when you take a step, any step, and see what happens.

This doesn't mean you are passively blown around by whims or external events; rather, you listen with all of your being and follow where you are called. It's about dedication and a deep desire to be who you truly are. Motivational speakers often suggest you can be anything you want to be if you believe in yourself, work hard, and go for it. From a Buddhist perspective, we don't focus on believing in "ourself," or trying to "become something." Rather, we let go of the ego self and allow our aliveness to arise within and lead us on the journey.

Leaping into space is a paradox of both going somewhere and going nowhere. We are going nowhere because there is nowhere to go. There's just the awakening of this moment.

Tung-shan asked: "Where are you going?"

Pen-shi answered: "I'm going to a changeless place."

Tung-shan said: "If it's a changeless place you won't be going there."

Pen-chi replied: "Going is also changeless."

—TSAO-SHAN, THE ROARING STREAM

55. Give Up a Timetable for Letting Go, Then Take Action

Letting go happens in its own time. We can be dedicated to our daily practice of inner attunement in whatever form it takes—meditation, exercise, journaling, music, movement, or quiet time and watch with fascination as life takes its course. We can go to a therapist, or a support group and read about forgiveness, but sometimes hurt, resentment, fear, or pain seem to cling. We can't will the stuck places to release at any given moment. Paradoxically, many people find a way to let go through their actions as opposed to hoping, praying, or wishing something would stop haunting them.

For example, Laura worked as an executive in a tall office building in midtown Manhattan. She became increasingly upset when the security guard by the elevator appeared hostile and unresponsive to her friendly hellos. Laura's head started swimming with negative thoughts about herself: "Why doesn't he like me? What have I done wrong?" As weeks went by, her whole body would tense up as she walked into the building. She chided herself, "Why am I letting this bother me so much? I'm getting completely undone by this man. I've even gotten so I dread going to work."

Then, finally, it occurred to her to say something about it to a friend at the office. She was tremendously relieved when her friend immediately responded that she too was troubled by his coldness and apparent hostility. Another person overheard and joined the conversation. She had also been upset by him. "It was amazing how talking about it cleared away all the horrible thoughts," Laura told me. The next day, when they talked about their intense feelings, they imagined all the trouble he might have in his life. They all agreed to be warm toward him no matter what his reaction. Everything changed. Laura was no longer afraid, and after a while he started being just a bit friendlier—at least that's how it seemed.

Laura's story illustrates many aspects of letting go: she reflected on her part in the situation, talked with others, and was able to shift from a childlike state of fear to an adult state of awareness. *It wasn't that she willed herself to "let go"; it was by talking with others that her mind let go and she was able to come back into current time and see clearly in reality.* That's a very important distinction. The mind often lets go of its obsessing when we take action to speak the truth or face reality.

Here are some ways to help with letting go in relationships:

1. **Clear up "unfinished business."** Unfinished business means feeling guilty, upset, unclear, or hurt, either by your actions toward others or from behavior directed at you. Decide if you need to talk, write a letter, make a phone call, or get help processing the situation.

2. **Ask for guidance.** If you can't get clear in a relationship, process your thoughts and feelings with a neutral, insightful friend, counselor, or therapist. Look at your part. Are you in a childlike fear or dependency state, or are you seeing clearly in reality? What feels true for you? Once you are in current time, you will know what to say.

3. **Make apologies whenever appropriate.** Scan your past and think of situations in which you feel badly about your behavior or know you hurt someone. To make a genuine apology you need to resonate with the person you hurt. Imagine the impact of your behavior by pretending you are that individual. You may need to

talk with others to understand the full impact of your behavior. When the time feels right, apologize by saying how you were either insensitive, unkind, thoughtless, or harmful. Do not start with excuses and reasons. Acknowledge the other person's hurt.

4. **Be comforted.** If you are in grief or pain over a loss, go to someone—talk, cry, be held, let yourself be cared for. Then take some time to tell the story of what you lost, what it meant to you, and what you learned.

5. **Say thank you.** Scan your past and think of ways in which people have been helpful or kind to you and thank them in some meaningful way. Gratitude is one of the highest vibrations of energy.

6. **Do not re-hash the same situation if it's getting nowhere.** Instead, take a break so both individuals can get clear for themselves and are able to be more forthright and honest. Endless processing is usually about not wanting to face some part of reality. When people are clear, conversations usually are brief.

7. **Let go of pressuring another person to agree with you.** In some situations there never will be agreement. You need to separate your pride from your desire for the relationship and decide what feels true for you. If you decide to proceed, you could start by asking "What's the next step?" or "What would you like from me?" or "Here's what I need from you." You agree that there is a different perception or belief.

8. **Create a ritual for letting go.** Sometimes we need to let go of grief or hurt from a person who is unwilling to talk with us or who is dead.

A touching example came from a dear cousin of mine. Ed, in his late forties, routinely fell into a deep depression just before Christmas. Ed's wife put together the pieces and figured out that the depression usually started near the anniversary of his mother's death. Ed realized that he had never truly grieved his mother, who died when he was in high school. His father had a stoic, hold-yourself-together kind of attitude, and life had moved on, leaving Ed's grief still churning inside.

To create a ritual, Ed asked relatives and friends who knew his mother to write stories about her and send them to him. Then, on the anniversary of her death, Ed explained to his two sons that he wanted to set aside a special time with them and his wife to talk about his mother because he had never grieved her death. He hoped it would help ease his chronic Christmas depression. On December 21, the family gathered together in the living room, lit candles, read what people had written, watched some old home movies, and provided Ed with a loving place to share memories of his mother.

"I can't say there was a sudden change in my depression," Ed said, "but there was some kind of shift over time. Gathering to talk about my mother became a yearly ritual, and everyone accepted it and took part. But then, one year, I didn't feel the need for it anymore. I was done."

Like Laura, Ed didn't set a timetable—he followed his instincts, took action, and the grief and depression let go in their own time.

56. Let Go of the Outcome

Many of us make leaps of faith without realizing it. We make most decisions with insufficient data. We go to a movie not knowing if we'll like it. We conceive a child without knowing what he'll be like. We try out a medical treatment without knowing if it will help—we might go through tremendous pain and discomfort and then get well, or we might not. We constantly choose between one path or another, not knowing what we really are choosing. You have probably already let go in hundreds of ways throughout your lifetime. The task for staying unstuck is to stay unattached to the outcome and not look back with regret.

Everything turns out one way or another; it's just the way it is. You can have a loosely held preference without creating turmoil inside. You can say, well, I really wanted to have that work out, without saying it was bad and unfair that it didn't. Life *is* unfair and lots of plans won't go as we expect.

You can still use a blueprint to build a house or practice diligently to play an instrument, but it's when your hands or breath sensuously shape a beautiful phrase and the sound soaks into your body and you and the instrument become the music that you dwell in experience. If you're practicing an instrument with your mind pointed toward a coming performance, you may feel an edge of anxiety that interferes with your ability to relax into the music. If you immerse yourself in the melodies, rhythm, and harmony, you become one with them.

Letting go of the outcome means being easy with yourself no matter what happens. You just spent eight dollars on a lousy movie, the dream job became more of a nightmare, the relationship was a big mistake, the cancer treatment didn't work. Have your feelings, but don't be hard on yourself. All we can do is step from one moment to the next, make our best decision with what we know, and breathe.

Some people who were faced with the possible loss of their homes during recent summer fires blazing around Missoula were intensely agitated with worry and couldn't function, while others moved their valuables to a storage shed and were able to proceed with life amid the uncertainty. They were able to let go of their attachment to their homes and possessions. One man said, "We've had eleven lovely years amid these beautiful pine trees and we've always known there was a chance of fire. But if the house burns down I'll never regret having lived here."

When we can say, "Yes, it's been lovely, and it may all burn down any moment," we are free. This applies to our beliefs, possessions, loved ones, work, and health. Our house may burn, we may have an accident, lose someone we love, or face a life-threatening illness. The more we can breathe into an experience, be totally with it and let it burn to ashes, the more we are ready for the final step of letting go, that mystery called death.

Breathing Exercise

1. Take a full, deep breath. Do this anytime you're suddenly disappointed, hurt, upset, or starting to defend or argue. Soften your belly, relax your shoulders, take a breath, and fully exhale. Breathe deeply again into the belly, slowly exhale and stay at the "bottom" of the breath, without immediately inhaling.

2. Sit with a straight back, soften your belly, and relax your shoulders. Repeat each one five or six times.

- Breathe in through the nose and out through the nose.
- Breathe in through the nose and out through the mouth.
- Breathe in through the mouth and out through the nose.
- Breathe in through the mouth and out through the mouth.
- Come back to your regular breathing.

Variation: Focus on your third eye—the spot located on your lower forehead above your eyes—while you do these breathing exercises.

3. A breathing exercise taught by the Sufi teacher Shabda Kahn.

- Breathe into your belly and abdomen for four counts.
- Hold your breath for four counts.
- Exhale slowly for four counts.
- Pause for four counts before repeating.

57. Let the Moment Burn to Ashes

Zen activity is activity which is completely burned out,
with nothing remaining but ashes.
—SHUNRYU SUZUKI, ZEN MIND, BEGINNER'S MIND

In Zen meditation, there is no goal. You meditate and see what happens. Likewise, when you take on an activity or project, you can give it your full attention and see what happens. It might be fun, easy, difficult, or unpleasant, and it will work out or it won't—it really doesn't matter. The task is to let ourselves become fully immersed in the moment.

Here is Jamie's story of letting old fears burn to ashes: "My teen-age daughter, Penny, asked me to buy a pet rat. My immediate answer was, 'Hell No! There's not going to be a rat in this house!' I was adamant. Months later, at Christmastime, feeling loving toward Penny, I asked, 'What can I give you for Christmas?' When she said 'a pet rat,' I could feel the flares rising, but I took a breath and calmed down. 'What is this huge fear and tension?' I wondered. I wanted to please her so much that we went to the pet store and I had them put the rat in my sweating, shaking hand. I could start to feel the softness of the white fur and the little heart beating, and I looked in its funny eyes.

"Then a thought came to me, 'You can love anything you're not afraid of.' So this furry rat came into our lives and when Penny moved away, the rat stayed and would come and sit on my shoulder when I read. I often remember that thought, 'You can love anything you're not afraid of.'"

What Jamie's story shows so beautifully is that letting go of fear can mean walking right into it with trembling hands and a rigid body. It also shows how love can help override intense fear, or literally burn it to ashes. Whatever had caused Jamie's body to seize up at the thought of having a pet rat was no longer related to the reality of this little rat she was petting. Through her own effort, and with the grace of love, her fear had burned to ashes.

Nostalgia for the past also keeps us from being in the present. When we try to duplicate an old experience—from love-making, to the perfect summer picnic, to a gathering of friends, to a holiday ritual—it might feel good, or it can fall flat. *Freedom means we can choose to do our traditional rituals or not.* Jenny, a single mom of three children, was exhausted at the prospect of preparing their traditional Christmas eve dinner. She said, "Hey, let's send out for Chinese food and skip all the rest." They lit candles and sat together in the living room; they ate on paper plates so there was no work. She remembered that Christmas as a wonderful day and evening with lots of time to relax and play games. It became a tradition.

Relationships often suffer when couples try to replicate a lovely experience. The story of Julia and Jim, who were engaged to be married, is a common one. Julia described a time of love-making as particularly tender, passionate, and warm. "I thought about it all week and looked forward to the coming Friday when we'd be together again. I imagined Jim arriving with flowers and complimenting me on the candlelit atmosphere and lovely food. I imagined us eating, talking for a long time, then touching and making love."

In reality, Jim showed up feeling tired and grouchy, asked her to turn up the lights because it was too dark, and wanted to unload about work. "I felt so let down that I couldn't listen to him—like a little kid who couldn't go to the carnival. He could tell I wasn't really hearing him, so he just stopped talking and shut down. The evening went dead."

Julia later came to realize she had created a scenario and had written Jim's lines with no regard for his reality. It was like saying, "Come be in my universe, be my puppet," instead of being open to letting the evening evolve. Jim added to the conversation: "When I saw how hurt Julia was, I felt like I was this terrible person. Not only did I blow it at work, but now I was making Julia upset. I knew at that point I wouldn't be able to make love. I really did look forward to seeing her, but when I walked in her apartment it felt like walking into a stage set, and something in me resisted. It's hard to explain."

Most people resist fitting into someone else's universe, to being a character in their play, unseen and unknown, just reading their lines. The candlelight and roses weren't the problem; it was Julia's underlying agenda that prevented her from yielding to the reality of Jim's actual situation. If she could have let go of her script for the evening and responded to the Jim who walked in the door, he could have felt understood and the evening might have been more loving. Likewise, Jim could have shown his appreciation and said, "This looks nice, but right now I need to sound off about work and just be quiet for a few minutes!" When he saw her hurt face he could have said, "Julia, I did not mean to hurt you; I want us to be together, but not with some set plan in mind." The ensuing resentment and hurt kept the experience burning for days because both had been caught up in an image instead of being real with each other.

A video of the Dalai Lama showed an incredible example of creating something beautiful and letting it go. As part of a Tibetan Buddhist ritual a group of monks work diligently for many days to create a Kalachakra sand mandala of incredible detail and beauty. (To see a picture, search for Kalachakra mandala on the internet.) In the next scene, the Dalai Lama, surrounded by several other monks, gives a loving look at the mandala, then runs his fingers through it. The others join in. Handfuls of the sand are given to observers as a peace offering. Then the monks carefully pour the remaining sand into an urn and from a small boat they slowly tip the urn and watch the sand stream into the river. Hello, you're beautiful, good bye. Impermanence.

58. Remember, You Are Not the "Doer"

> *Those who pursue learning daily increase results. Those who have heard the tao daily drop something. They decrease until they arrive at a point of non-doing. In doing nothing there is nothing left undone.*
>
> —TAO-TE CHING, VERSE 48

Letting go takes you from do-ing to a sense of non-doing. What you drop on a daily basis is your ego identification with your actions, beliefs, talents, and weaknesses. This frees you to follow the flow of life as it pulses through you. This doesn't mean inaction; it means that motion comes through fascination, interest, and a flow that is part of something bigger. In the movie *Chariots of Fire*, about track athletes from the British Isles who ran in the 1924 Olympics, Eric Liddell, a central character, says, "God made me fast. When I run, I feel his pleasure." It's like running and not being the runner.

In *Alice in Wonderland*, there are various phrases such as "*I found myself* walking in a beautiful garden." Have you ever felt ambivalent about going to a gathering or going on an excursion, then *found* yourself getting dressed and thinking, "I guess I'm going"?

Martin tells this story: "Mary and I had been living together for three years in the best relationship I've ever had. One day, while we were hanging out downtown we wandered in a jewelry store to look around. We stopped at the display of wedding rings and pointed out the ones we liked, then even tried a couple of them on. Then we glanced up and gave a knowing smile to each other because we knew it meant we'd get married. It's as if I noticed what we were doing and saw what it told us rather than the other way around. It just happened."

Instead of thinking of yourself as the doer, consider that you are the channel, the messenger, the vehicle of consciousness, part of the stream of All That Is. Imagine yourself like a single cell in a body. You are intrinsic to the whole, and your moment to moment experience results from a vast web of interconnections. If you get a little cut or burn, "it" heals. The body moves to action; you don't "do" it. You can help the healing with ice or ointments, but you are just the helper.

When you walk through a shopping area, do you ever "find yourself" pulled in one direction or another? Let's say you are attracted to a blue shirt you see in a window. You might say, "I'm drawn to it because I like blue." But then, as Nisargadatta teaches, turn your attention around inside and ask, "Who is this 'I' who likes blue?" "Who is this 'I' who likes this type of shirt?" Then everything starts to dissolve.

Play with this statement in your mind: "*I am upset with myself.*" Who is this "I" and who is the "myself"? Often the "I" we perceive is the ego judging the actions of the "myself." In contrast, when you do something for the pure joy, excitement, beauty, or love of doing it without an agenda for praise or accomplishment, then you are in the flow of consciousness. You are not the doer; you are part of a vortex of energy in motion.

Rabbi David Zeller has written a song called "I Am Alive!" with a melody that's rhythmic, energetic, and fun to dance to:

Lai lai lai lai lai lai lai lai, I am alive
Lai lai lai lai lai lai lai lai, I am alive
And who is this aliveness I am?
And who is this aliveness I am?
And who is this aliveness I am?
Is it not the Holy Blessed One?

We *are* the aliveness that has no form, no center, no identity. To be unstuck and free is to align ourselves with the aliveness that we are—to feel it, dance with it, be it, and let it carry us.

59. Be Willing to Let Go When the Passion Fades

Just because you have a talent for something doesn't mean you are obliged to do it forever or that the form can't change. I'm speaking of letting go when something you love starts to become a burden or is drained of its life-giving spark. I'll never forget that wrenching moment when I gazed around my music studio at Ohio University for the last time, ran my fingers over the keys of the Steinway grand pianos, closed the door, and left what I had once thought would be my life's work as a piano instructor. I was done.

I walked down the corridor, left the music building, and crossed a side street to the counseling department, where I would soon be a full-time student. My new "office" was one of four desks set in a cramped space with no windows, but it was part of a whole new world about to open to me as a teaching assistant in the counseling department.

There comes a moment when we know we're done, finished—something has burned to ashes all on its own. Our challenge is to let it go even if it means giving up status, security, the familiar, or winning the race.

Doug Swingley won the Iditarod four times and appeared likely to win a fifth. The Iditarod is an Alaskan sled dog race and the gold standard for mushing; it takes a minimum of nine days to complete. Doug, who loved dog sledding, and is an incredibly talented musher, decided to back away when the experience no longer brought joy to him. In spite of perfect snow and an excellent team of dogs, he had held back his competitive instincts, slowed down the pace, and fell to the back of the competitors as his way of bowing out of the race. He dropped from first to fortieth, took thirteen days instead of nine, and won just over a thousand dollars—after his previous win of over sixty-two thousand.

"I have never gotten to run a fun Iditarod just to relax and visit with the people," he was quoted as saying in the local paper, *The Missoulian*. He wanted to take a victory lap and enjoy the scenery with long breaks along the way. "I'm having a blast," he continued. "The leisurely pace has made it feel like the first time up the trail. The fact that I'm tired of competing in the Iditarod has to do with a lot of things. The media, remarks from my competitors, Alaskans' snide remarks. I don't enjoy that part at all. So the easiest thing is to back away from it." Along with the newspaper article was a marvelous picture of Doug standing in the snow alongside his sled dogs, radiating happiness. He had won the bigger race—he stayed true to himself.

It may seem simple to say that we should stop pushing ourselves if we don't enjoy the race any longer. But why not? It may hit a nerve inside that goes counter to the puritan ethics that extol hard work, suffering, security, and virtue. Or it may go against the inflated ego that says going for the gold, winning, and getting accolades make us important. But imagine if you left the ghost of your conditioning behind and allowed yourself to come into current time and resonate with your whole being so you can make decisions from a place inside that feels like fresh air. From this place it's easy to step out of the race, slow down, watch the scenery, and talk to the people along the trail.

I've interviewed people who stepped down from high status jobs, left teaching, or got out of the game when it no longer felt good. Stephen Wolinsky stopped teaching introductory workshops a few years ago. When asked why, he answered simply, "I'm done." When pressed for reasons, he said, "I could make up a story, but the truth is, I'm just done, nothing in me wants to do it anymore."

When something that once felt fun, fresh, exciting, and new fades, and nothing revitalizes it, we are wise to let it go. To keep at it can feel like trying to keep a dying person alive against their will. This can be a daunting challenge, especially when it involves major changes in life, but staying unstuck and breaking free means we go where there's fresh air in our lives. Sometimes with rest, an old love takes a new form and we return with renewed vitality, but sometimes it slips away and is gone forever.

60. Be Willing to Let Go of Comfort

In the United States we are incredibly attached to comfort—to warm homes, high-tech clothes, shoes for every occasion, availability of foods from anyplace in the world, automatic doors, quick check-out lines, instant loans, and fast service. The paradox is that the more we feel entitled to conveniences, the more impatient we get when things go wrong. It's as if our nervous systems are permanently revved up so it becomes difficult to relax when we have to wait or we can't have what we want . . . immediately! We sometimes become like demanding children who pout, whine, or complain when things don't go our way. Our impatience disturbs our peace of mind and transmits agitation to everyone around us.

Oprah Winfrey recently took a trip to South Africa to give presents to 50,000 children. When I watched the account I was particularly intrigued by the innocent, open, smiling faces of the children and how much less restless and jaded they seemed than many children from the United States. Oprah spoke of wanting to give them something and to be of service, but my thought was that we have a lot to learn from those children who appeared so polite and good to each other.

These children are clearly suffering in many ways from the profound impact of AIDS and poverty. But they have a richness that comes from non-attachment, community values, and happiness.

One woman on Oprah's staff, breaking down in tears, said, "Look at how completely happy this child is to be given one good pair of shoes while I probably have fifteen pairs in my closet." Exactly. We need to cry for our excesses because they often reflect our unhappiness. The happiness quotient between no shoes and one pair of shoes is far greater than any succeeding pairs we add to the collection.

There is something profound in having just enough, but not more than we need; of treasuring our resources and being willing to accommodate for a greater good. During the oil crisis Jimmy Carter addressed the country sitting in a heavy sweater by a fire in the White House. He said that we all needed to pull together, and that if everyone would turn their thermostats down by three or four degrees in the daytime and more at night it would make a huge difference. This was so little to ask, yet many people in the United States would consider this a major burden—they don't want to feel a chill in the air when they wake up or give up using their gas-guzzling vehicles to drive to the corner store for a latte whenever they desire.

A woman who rents out rooms in her home recently told me, "I tell prospective renters that I keep the house a bit cool in winter—that I heat for sweatshirts and sweatpants. You'd be amazed how many people feel that it's an affront to their personal comfort and are unwilling to live under such conditions. They seem to have no understanding that it's not just about their right to wear T-shirts and shorts in winter; it's about oil, and drilling in the Arctic refuge, and war, and preserving resources for the next generation." Being unstuck is about having a spacious heart that connects far and wide beyond *my* needs, *my* rights, and *my* way of life. It's knowing that there is one life, and we're all part of it.

Letting go of comfort is also a prime ingredient in adventure and learning. A friend of mine completed a sprint triathalon despite being very anxious about swimming in a deep lake—she had an irrational but very real fear that dragons might come up and grab her.

She swam it anyway and plans to do the triathalon again next year because of the sense of elation and accomplishment it brought. Children don't demand comfort until we teach them to. Youngsters at an ice skating rink are willing to fall down and get up hundreds of times because of their strong desire to skate. Adults would do well to follow their lead. Think of something you want enough to be willing to struggle for, be uncomfortable with, and keep coming back a hundred times.

Millie described the first time she was invited on a camping trip: "I was very uneasy when I thought about not having all my things with me—my warm bed, a stove, a choice of books to read—all the stuff that makes me feel safe and comfortable. I worried about bug bites, being cold, wet, and hungry. It was a looming fear that I'd be miserable and unable to escape, and it took great effort to rouse myself to go, which I did mostly because I enjoyed being with my friends.

"The surprise was that I soon realized I could be just fine without all my little comforts. I watched my friends light up the small Coleman stove and make great food. I think I had this image that we'd be eating grits or beans while standing in the rain, freezing. Not only did I start to feel comfortable; after a while I felt a lovely kind of freedom. The simplicity of having just what you need while enjoying the beauty of the mountains and the hikes became a gift, not an ordeal."

It is not wrong to enjoy being comfortable. But notice if you allow a fear of being uncomfortable stand in the way of doing things that would take your life forward. Do you sometimes choose comfort and familiar rituals over having a new experience or adventures that might expand your life in countless ways or help others?

The Long Walk by Slavomir Rawicz gives a stark perspective on the immense demands we make for comfort. In 1941, Slavomir and a small group of fellow prisoners escaped a Soviet labor camp with nothing more than an axe, a knife, and minimal food. Their year-long walk to India included the Siberian Arctic, the Gobi Desert, and the Himalayas. They often went for days at a time hiking twenty miles without water or food. Throughout the ordeal they treated one another with immense respect—no one person hoarded food for themselves and they talked over all their plans, coming to consensus before taking action. Their ability to stay unified as a group may well have been what kept them alive and able to tolerate their immense suffering through cold, heat, near starvation, sleep deprivation, and thirst. No one ever spoke of hopelessness or the possibility they wouldn't make it. Every ounce of their energy was directed toward survival.

> *Live simply so that others may simply live.*
> —QUAKER SAYING

On the journey to being unstuck, we need to be willing to adapt, change, and remember that for some people to have the bare necessities means others need to relinquish some of their comforts and conveniences. Every time you pick up an item made in a developing country, take a moment to imagine the person who made it—the woman repeatedly sewing the same seam hour after hour or straining her eyes to wire up a calculator that you can buy for under ten dollars. Think of the exhaustion of working long hours for little pay, the poverty, the effect on her home life. Then picture the people who have profited by her hard labor, including you and me. Send everyone a prayer that they find happiness and the root of all happiness; that they know kindness and the root of all kindness. Do whatever you can to realize your connection with your brothers and sisters everywhere. Going a step further, think of ways to take action to change these inequities.

61. Feel the Friendliness of Freedom

> *You are the fountain of the sun's light*
> *I am a willow shadow on the ground*
> *You make my raggedness silky.*
> —RUMI, *THE ESSENTIAL RUMI*

Some of the true signs of being unstuck are friendliness, light-heartedness, receptivity, and joy. It's a friendliness born of aliveness, awe, and fascination. You become able to look kindly into the eyes of others without fear because there's nothing in the way—no shame, judgments, secrets, or agitation. Authentic warmth and friendliness are hallmarks of people who are free in their hearts and in their lives.

Have you ever noticed that when you are in a relaxed, generous, open-hearted state fear slips away and you can more easily reach out to others, be forgiving, and be able to listen without the ego constantly interrupting to talk about yourself? As we let go and fall in love with life, we radiate what lovers feel.

For nearly fifty years the Buddha taught those who would listen. He was both rational, practical, and tender—a cool head and a warm heart. He never positioned himself as being other than human and was admittedly fallible and open to criticism. He was known to say, "I summon you, disciples, to tell me: have you any fault to find with me in word or in deed?" His compassion and kindness toward others became deeply embedded in his message.

While watching a video of the His Holiness the Dalai Lama I was struck by his laughter, warmth, and friendliness as he reached out to people with no perceptible barrier in between. When someone would ask why a certain healing happened or wanted reasons for this or that, he often smiled, pondered for a moment, then said, "I don't know," shrugged his shoulders, and laughed. He lives beyond the stories, the analysis, the reasons why, just as the Buddha did. Yet similar to the Buddha he is drawn to scientific studies and quantum physics, which help us understand the nature of reality. He raises money to help people from Tibet and is dedicated to his meditation practice.

When you are awake and alive, the message is in your being—the steadiness, friendliness, honesty, and kindness you radiate in the world. This is not to portray a kind of syrupy sweetness often associated with "enlightenment." Rather, you become real and respond to the moment from the core of your being, seeing through the superficial coverings into the hearts of others.

> Friend, our closeness is this:
> anywhere you put your foot, feel me
> in the firmness under you.
>
> How is it with this love,
> I see your world and not you?
> —RUMI, THE ESSENTIAL RUMI

62. Let Go of Self and Come into the Spirit of Life

The only true happiness is knowing who we are—feeling an unbounded, deeply awakened love consciousness. The concept of being born again is to me an awaking from a feeling of separateness. I imagine people in slow motion, immersing themselves in a beautiful lake or river, then coming up, taking a breath, and awakening to the realization of how awesome, unbounded, and connected it all is—the water, sky, air, the ability to breathe, and this body we live in. In tribal communities no one is alone—everyone is an integral part of the whole and people are encouraged to develop their particular talents and strengths so they can give their best to the community. Our talents and strengths are not just personal attributes; they are life moving through us—something to enjoy *and* to give away.

As we come to experience ourselves as part of one endless thread woven together into the fabric of existence, our inner experience of living shifts dramatically. Along with becoming more relaxed, we all become visionaries for creating a more just, equitable, and peaceful society. Being guided by this reality is to live as the Buddha, with compassion and kindness for all. As a result, we realize that to live out of balance with the earth, animals, and all sentient life ricochets back on us. The elements that sustain life, such as clean air, water, healthy vegetation, and the ozone are not bounded by countries, religion, or ethnicity. To a person who is truly alive, these elements become more precious than gold, status, or power. They are life itself.

Jesus' words, "When you do it to the least of us you do it unto me," also reflect the consciousness of the Buddha. Love is not a special feeling we save for family and friends; it is the embodiment of a heart open to the suffering and joys of all people. There is no "other," only our reflection in a thousand mirrors.

We create peace in this world through accepting ourselves fully and bringing our full aliveness to whatever we do and whatever we are, softening the barriers between ourselves and others. Our perception of an integrated world becomes reflected in a circular relationship with our inner experience. Said another way, our view of a fragmented world reflects the divisions within us. When we have a fluid, unified experience of body, mind, and spirit it is reflected in a unified perception of all sentient life.

We started our journey by leaving home and venturing forth into the world to find our dreams, which was really about finding the aliveness that we are. We faced hazards and trials as we met up with trixters, sages, and other people just like us wandering around looking for a nameless something to ease their pain or anxiety and give life meaning and joy. We explored a legion of ways to find excitement, happiness, and meaning and were given many promises and suggestions about what would work. Sometimes we got useful pieces of the puzzle; other times the teachings took us off course and they inflated the sense of "I" instead of helping it recede. We may have acquired ideas, possessions, adventures, and knowledge, but something still remained restless or empty and hungry.

Eventually we realize that we are always home; we just forget that the journey lies within us, beyond any concepts of doing and achieving. It is in letting go of our identification with our separate self, the "I" who has been doing all the seeking. As the "I" recedes, we became grounded in essence rather than in our beliefs or images about who we are. We start to experience an unbounded deep awakened love consciousness.

As the past dissolves and beliefs fade, we find ourselves in the wonderous world of beingness or essence. In this place, love, creativity, and kindness are natural. They are not out there; they are in here—they flow within us and between us without effort. From this place we can develop our gifts and talents as contributing members of our community—as a healthy, vital cell in the organism of all life.

I recently sang in a performance of George Frideric Handel's *Messiah* to raise money for Missoula's Habitat for Humanity Organization, a group that helps finance and build homes for low income people. The soloists, conductor, orchestra, and chorus all volunteered their time. In addition, each member of the chorus raised fifty dollars in order to sing in the choir. The excitement was palpable on the evening of the concert. The chorus gathered for the warm-up, the orchestra members pulled out their instruments, and people started streaming into the large university theater—a full house.

As we gathered on stage, I watched the orchestra tuning up and imagined each one of them as a child, having their first music lesson—

the scratchy bow, the little fingers on the keyboard, pursing one's lips to make a sound come out of a wind instrument. I imagined all the vocal training, experience in choirs, or singing at home with family that resulted in this resonant, full-voiced chorale. I then fast-forwarded through countless hours of collective practicing—maybe millions of hours—and persevering that led to everyone walking onto the stage this night.

But now, silence. The mind stops and the music begins. The conductor lifts his baton, and after a vibrant hush we become one orchestra, one chorus, and one performance of this glorious music. A thrill goes through the full auditorium. There are no concepts to divide us, no thoughts to distract us. As each one becomes a channel for the melodies and words, we come into the whole, the play of consciousness where the notes become music. This is the world of freedom—bringing our gifts together to enjoy and give away. No grasping, no holding on. Just bringing our full attention to what we are doing, and when we are done, we go home. But we are forever changed—while the performance is over, the music now lives within us.

Take time to feel the aliveness within you, appreciate the story of your very special life, nurture the gifts you have been given, and bring them into your community. When we are connected to each other yet not identified with our separate selves, our hearts expand into the unified field of All That Is, the indivisible essence of life, the heart of the Beloved. In this place of aliveness there is no suffering.

With love and all best wishes,
Your sister,
Charlotte Sophia
Lolo, Montana

Afterword

I t became something of a joke with my friends that I got stuck
writing a book on getting unstuck. It took less than a week to
write the proposal that I envisioned becoming a manageable six
month project. More than two and a half years have passed since
then. But, as my friend and occasional writing teacher, David James
Duncan, said, "Writing a book on getting unstuck is really asking for
it!" For sure.

While I definitely got lost, disorganized, sidetracked, overly abstract, discouraged, and waylaid with a barrage of life events, there
was something else that made this book a challenge. Namely, the subject kept going deeper and deeper within me, like quicksand pulling
out my footing, causing me to reconsider or change my perspective. I
spoke with many people, read, listened to tapes, went to retreats, observed, and let my own stuck places be mirrored back to me.

I feel as if I've lived every word of this book and know more
deeply what it feels like to lose confidence and get lost, and also what
it means to climb out of a hole. From a writing perspective, it's been
about persevering *and* relaxing, carefully polishing something yet
being willing to throw it away, working harder *and* taking time out
for fun or relaxation. It's also been about asking for help.

After a lukewarm response to my second version of the book, I
said to my agent of seventeen years, "How can this happen? I
thought it was better than that." "It just happens," she said. "It can
happen to anyone. It will be all right." I was soothed but wondered if
I was losing my radar or my writing instincts. I had liked the way I
ended the book, but no one else did.

Then, at the suggestion of my editor, I hired what's known in the trade as a "book doctor." I groaned at the expense, but I now think of her as the shepherd who brought great skill and kindness in guiding me through to the final step. She assured me that the only content problem was having too much. What I needed was organization, to make connections for the reader, and to be more direct and concrete.

I was barraged over and over with a string of sudden events that totally stopped my writing. There was the sudden death of my partner's two nephews; the many neighborhood meetings to stave off a proposed housing development in the field below us; the car tire mistakenly put in the back of my minivan that flew out, whacked my knee, tore the ligament, wrenched my hip, and left me lying around with ice packs, and which has required doctor visits, Rolfing, and physical therapy.

Last summer, the threat of nearby forest fires and evacuation warnings meant getting help to "make my house defensible." I felt deeply moved by all the people who arrived to help me complete a long list of tasks that included raking every pine needle within thirty to forty feet of the house, getting the wood pile and scraps away from the base of the house, and (tears again) pulling up my treasured young pine grove on the hill by my house that my cousin said would act like little torches to set off my house.

There was also the task of packing boxes to take to a storage shelter—photographs, paintings, important papers, and pictures. I pondered about what mattered. I'd walk around the house enjoying the sunlight streaming in, treasuring the rocks and woodwork and touching the walls and various objects. And at the same time I'd be saying, "I'll be all right, I can live without it." I was immensely relieved when my morning hiking area was spared from the fire that burned up to its edge. To my surprise I heard myself think, "I'd rather lose my house than this beautiful hiking area." Then, finally, it rained, cool weather set in, the fires subsided, the air cleared, and it was all yesterday's news. Just a lot of boxes to bring home and unpack.

The deepest stuck place was when I lost my writing voice, which felt like losing my best friend—a bright clear place in my head that delights and guides me and pops up with all kinds of ideas. Walking aimlessly around in the Goodwill one morning the sharp searing reality hit full force—I needed to leave my primary relationship. Even when I could concentrate, my writing was fractured and mushy. After the separation, as the brain fog gradually lifted, I wondered how many people were sacrificing their brilliance, creativity, and clarity to hold onto a relationship that wasn't working. Regaining the clarity of my voice felt as if I had found my true lover—the aliveness within me. It took a long time.

Sometimes I would say to myself, "Everything that's happening is life; I need to be present to whatever is going on." But another part would say, "What a pain in the butt to get so lost and have all these interruptions." Then, I would fly out into "big mind" and think about the people in Africa who have AIDS, the homeless children, the people in Baghdad or Afghanistan, women being battered, the torment of sexual slavery, or people around the globe living without adequate food, clean water, and, most of all, safety. Holding to this view became a profound challenge when faced with the recent news that my daughter was diagnosed with liver cancer. As I prepare to send this manuscript in later today, my daughter and I are planning a trip to a Club Med that we went to twenty-two years ago when she was in seventh grade. After that she'll start chemotherapy.

Tonglin meditation has become my daily practice—it helps reduce my challenges to something like dust on the floor. I'll think to myself, I am so lucky, I've had so much help to feel stable inside. I *do* have food, friends, a warm bed, and access to good health care. I can go to a physical therapist instead of limping for the rest of my life, I belong to a health club, I've got it easy. Even if they don't accept this book or I have to give the money back, it's so small.

While I have longed for more time to play the piano, hike, and see friends, there have been many moments of being unstuck: in protest of aging, I increased my morning workouts and did a sprint triatha-lon with three women friends. I got a medal as a result of being the only one in my age category—endurance finally won out! I avoided my usual writing weight gain, and with the help of Weight Watchers and the South Beach Diet I lost nearly twenty pounds. I've also hiked, canoed, and camped in these magnificent mountains and rivers with wonderful friends and attended many fine workshops, concerts, and plays. In short, life happened, the book got written, and I learned a lot in the process and feel more prepared to face the future.

Toward the end of my first book in 1988, I wrote of a sweet young black female cat I found in the garage on a minus 20 degree day in Minnesota. I still have a vivid memory of picking her up and feeling all my stress drain away as she burrowed into my chest. Ruby was my writing companion for twelve years, nearly always sitting on top of the computer, bapping me when I'd brush her tail off the screen. She's buried on the hill behind my house. She wasn't around for this book.

Now I am sitting at the computer with a new kitty, Sally, nestled in my lap. A little calico girl. She could care less about all these words—she simply wants to snuggle up and be petted. I keep think-ing about the endless flow of sorrow and rejoicing, of gain and loss, that cycles through our lives, how to live with it, be part of it, yet let it all go, with amusement, love, and tenderness. This book has been my teacher; I hope it will speak to you as well.

Namaste,

Charlotte Sophia Kasl

Recommended Reading

Aslett, Don. *Clutter's Last Stand.*

Barks, Coleman, and A. J. Arberry, translator. *Like This: Rumi*

Barks, Coleman, and John Moyne, translator. *The Essential Rumi.*

———. *Say I Am You: Poetry Interspersed with Stories of Rumi and Shams.*

Bly, Robert. *The Kabir Book: Forty-four of the Ecstatic Poems of Kabir.*

Boorstein, Sylvia. *It's Easier Than You Think: The Buddhist Way to Happiness.*

Bunson, Matthew E. *The Wisdom Teachings of the Dalai Lama.*

Capra, Fritjof. *The Tao of Physics.*

———. *The Turning Point: Science, Society, and the Rising Culture.*

Chodron, Pema. *Start Where You Are: A Guide to Compassionate Living.*

———. *When Things Fall Apart: Heart Advice for Difficult Times.*

———. *The Wisdom of No Escape: And the Path of Loving-Kindness.*

Conze, Edward. *Buddhist Wisdom Books: The Diamond Sutra, The Heart Sutra.*

Das, Lama Surya. *Awakening the Buddha Within.*

Davis, Laura. *I Thought We'd Never Speak Again.*

Duncan, David James. *My Story as Told by Water.*

Easwaran, Eknath. *The Bhagavad Gita.*

Fromm, Erich. *The Art of Loving.*

Gandhi. *An Autobiography: The Story of My Experiments with Truth.*

Gibran, Kahlil. *The Prophet.*

Gilliam, Marianne. *How Alcoholics Anonymous Failed Me.*

Hafiz. *The Gift.* Translations by Daniel Ladinsky.

Hanh, Thich Nhat. *Commentaries on the Prajnaparamita Diamond Sutra.*

———. *The Diamond That Cuts Through Illusion.*

———. *The Heart of Understanding: Commentaries on the Prajnaparamita Heart Sutra.*

———. *Peace Is Every Step: The Path of Mindfulness in Everyday Life.*

Harrison, Steven. *Doing Nothing: Coming to the End of the Spiritual Search.*

Hawkins, M.D., Ph.D. Power vs. Force: The Hidden Determinants of Human Behavior.

Johnson, Susan M. Creating Connections.

———. Emotionally Focused Therapy for Trauma Survivors.

Kasl, Charlotte Sophia, Ph.D. Finding Joy: 101 Ways to Free Your Spirit and Dance with Life.

———. A Home for the Heart: Creating Intimacy with Loved Ones, Neighbors, and Friends.

———. If the Buddha Dated: A Handbook for Finding Love on a Spiritual Path.

———. If the Buddha Married: Creating Enduring Relationships on a Spiritual Path.

———. Many Roads, One Journey: Moving Beyond the Twelve Steps.

———. Women, Sex, and Addiction: A Search for Love and Power.

———. Yes, You Can! A Guide to Empowerment Groups. (Available via my website, charlottekasl.com, or by writing to Many Roads, One Journey, P.O. Box 1302, Lolo, MT 59847.)

Katagiri, Dainin. You Have to Say Something: Manifesting Zen Insight.

Keyes, Ken. Gathering Power Through Insight and Love.

———. Handbook to Higher Consciousness.

Krishnamurti, J. The Book of Life.

Levine, Peter A. Healing Trauma, audiotape, available through Sounds True.

———. Sexual Healing, audiotape available through Sounds True.

———. Waking the Tiger. (A body-centered approach to overcoming trauma.)

Linssen, Robert. Living Zen.

Miller, Jean Baker, M.D. Toward a New Psychology of Women.

Nisargadatta, Sri Maharaj. I Am That.

Ornish, Dean, M.D. Love & Survival: The Scientific Basis for the Healing Power of Intimacy.

Pert, Candace B., Ph.D. Molecules of Emotion: The Science Behind Mind-Body Medicine.

Rahula, Walpola. What the Buddha Taught.

Rawicz, Slavomir. The Long Walk: The True Story of a Trek to Freedom.

Suzuki, Daisetz Teitaro. Essays in Zen Buddhism.

Suzuki, Shunryu. Zen Mind, Beginner's Mind.

Von Oech, Roger. *A Whack on the Side of the Head: How You Can Be More Creative.*

Wolinsky, Stephen. *A Beginner's Guide to Quantum Psychology.*

————. *Hearts on Fire: The Tao of Meditation.*

————. *Quantum Consciousness: The Guide to Experiencing Quantum Psychology.*

————. *The Tao of Chaos: Quantum Consciousness.*

————. *The Way of the Human*, Volumes I, II, and III.

Resources

Cool Water Hula Video

To order Kristie Hager's video on the making of the Cool Water Hula, which includes the performance at the Berkeley Pit in Butte, Montana (see page 205), contact:

Cool Water Hula
430 East Spruce Street
Missoula, MT 59802
Price: $18.00 VHS; $25.00 DVD, including shipping

Intensive Psychotherapy

I (Charlotte Kasl) am available for intensive psychotherapy sessions for individuals and couples. These sessions take place in my office, near Missoula, Montana, and range in time from ten to twenty hours over a three- to five-day period. I use a combination of EMDR, ego state therapy, hypnosis, quantum psychology, and body movement awareness.

I approach couples therapy from an attachment model called Emotionally Focused Therapy (EFT), which comes from the teachings of Susan M. Johnson, author of *Creating Connections* and *Emotionally Focused Couples Therapy for Trauma Survivors*. EFT helps couples drop below the surface level so they're able to have heartfelt conversations connected to their emotions, the source of change. EFT focuses on naming and understanding the repetitive patterns in which couples get stuck, and moving toward the positive patterns that create intimacy, safety, and connection. I also add aspects of body movement to this therapy.

I have a Ph.D. from Ohio University and I am a licensed Clinical Professional Counselor in Montana and a Certified Addiction Specialist in the areas of chemical dependency and sexual relationships. You can go to my website, charlottekasl.com, for more information. My office phone number is listed below.

Therapy Referrals

Please note. I do not have referrals for therapists around the country.

My bias is for therapy that involves working to release the holding patterns in the body and nervous system and access emotions, especially when dealing with trauma, depression, and anxiety. For example, EMDR combined with ego-state therapy, or someone who works with body centered therapy. When you're seeking a therapist it is crucial to talk with them and ask questions to see if the person feels right for you. Even if the therapist has taken a particular training, they may not necessarily be appropriate for your needs.

EMDR (Eye Movement Desensitization and Reprocessing)

This is an advanced technology used for releasing traumatic memories, changing negative core beliefs and behavior patterns, and overcoming addictive and compulsive behavior. It is very focused, efficient, and effective and helps release the automatic physiological triggers of fear, anger, and hurt stemming from trauma. For more information you can read EMDR by Francine Shapiro (HarperCollins), or go to the EMDR or EMDRIA website. For a therapist in your area, or for information, write or call:

EMDR
P.O. Box 51010
Pacific Grove, CA 93950
Phone: (831) 372-3900
Fax: (831) 647-9881

Sensorimotor Psychotherapy

This is a form of body-centered therapy. See website on sensorimotor psychotherapy for articles and therapists near you. Pat Ogden is a particularly experienced sensorimotor therapist who gives trainings. You can reach her at:

P.O. Box 19438
Boulder, CO 80308
Phone: (302) 447-3290

You can go to her website, sensorimotorpsychotherapy.org, to read her sensorimotor psychotherapy articles and to learn about her trainings.

Sexual Addiction and Codependency

A good resource for therapists in this field is NCSAC, the National Council on Sexual Addiction and Compulsivity.

P.O. Box 725544
Atlanta, GA 31139
Phone: (770) 989-9754
NCSAC.org

Couples Therapy

For Emotionally Focused Therapy (EFT) referrals, you can contact:

Ottawa Couple & Family Institute
1869 Carling Avenue, Suite 201
Ottawa, Ontario, Canada KSA1E6
Phone: (613) 722-5122
ocfi@magma.ca

Correspondence

I love to receive letters and I read them all, but I can't promise to respond. If you'd like information on workshops, intensive therapy, 16-step empowerment groups, order forms for books, or various articles, you can go to my website, charlottekasl.com.

Trainings

I am available for workshops, talks, consulting, and therapist trainings on a variety of topics related to dating, relationships, creating joy, a 16-step empowerment model for healing from trauma and addiction, combining EMDR and ego-state therapy, and addressing core attachment issues. I also do workshops and talks on Buddhism and dating, relationships, psychotherapy and getting unstuck. I have a listing of sample workshops and descriptions on my website.

Charlotte Kasl
P.O. Box 1302
Lolo, MT 59847
Phone: (406) 273-6080
Fax: (406) 273-0111
www.charlottekasl.com
e-mail: charlottekasl@yahoo.com
NOTE: We do not check e-mail every day.

Grateful acknowledgment is made for permission to reprint excerpts from the following copyrighted works:

On This Night: 15 Dohas, versions by Coleman Barks (Maypop Books). By permission of Coleman Barks.

Doing Nothing: Coming to the end of the spiritual Search by Steven Harrison. Copyright © Steven Harrison, 1997. By permission of Jeremy P. Tarcher/Penguin, a member of Penguin Group (USA) Inc.

Zen Mind, Beginner's Mind by Shunryu Suzuki. By permission of Shambhala Publications, Inc.

Radical Ecstasy, adapted by Robert bly. Copyright © 2004 by Robert Bly. Reprinted by permission of Beacon Press, Boston.

I Am That: Talks with Sri Nisargadatta Maharaj. Translated from the Marathi recording by Maurice Frydman, edited by Sudhakar S. Dikshit. The Acorn Press, Durham, North Carolina, 1997.

Being Zen by Robert Lissner. By permission of Grove/Atlantic, Inc.

"Second Sun, 29," from *Sonnets to Orpheus* by Rainer Maria Rilke, translated by M.D. Herter Norton. Copyright 1942 by W. W. Norton & Company, Inc. renewed © 1970 by M. D. Herter Norton. Used by permission of W. W. Norton & Company, Inc.

The Gift, Poems by Hafiz, translations by Daniel Ladinsky (Penguin Compass). Copyright © 1999 by Daniel Ladinsky. Reprinted by permission of Daniel Ladinsky.

The Prophet by Kahlil Gibran. By permission of Alfred A. Knopf, a division of Random House, Inc.

Nonviolent Communication: A Language of Life by Marshall B. Rosenberg. Reprinted with permission of PuddleDancer Press.

"December 8," from *The Path to Tranquility* by The Dalai Lama, edited by Renuka Singh. Copyright © The Dalai Lama and Renuka Singh, 1998. Used by permission of Viking Penguin, a division of Penguin Group (USA) Inc.

Summer Meditation by Vaclav Havel. By permission of Vintage Books, a division of Random House, Inc.

"I Am Alive," translation by Rabbi David Zeller, a selection from *The Hidden Light of* the Eyes by Rabbi Menachem Nachum. By permission of Rabbi David Zeller (www.davidzeller.org).